"my fingers and my toes"

By James Larkin Pearson

"my fingers and my toes"

Complete Poems of
JAMES LARKIN PEARSON
Poet Laureate of North Carolina

Compiled and Promoted

By

Wilkes Community College

Wilkesboro, North Carolina

Ingram Book Company
Nashville, Tennessee
1971

Dedicated to
FAY CAUDLE BYRD
and
J. JAY ANDERSON
Staff Members of
Wilkes Community College
Wilkesboro, N. C.

CONTENTS

THE DREAM LIVES ON

INTRODUCTION

A book of the most comprehensive collection of poems of James Larkin Pearson is—like the complete work of any other poet who has devoted a lifetime to his craft—an autobiography. This is good, for Pearson is the sort of fellow we want to know, the sort of admirable man from whom we can learn some truths about living.

Furthermore, this collection provides us with a constant. In a day when fashions in poetry change every year, even sometimes every few months, we need to keep one of our hands on the immutable. We need to grasp something solid to let us know where we are.

The scene shifts, of course, as does time. First there are glimpses of Pearson's family. Then, long before his reminders of twentieth-century science and inventions, we learn about a mountain boyhood in an age not so sophisticated as ours. In these nostalgic pages from rural America in which Pearson is

> *Recallin' things we heard an' saw*
> *When we was kids a-burnin' straw,*

we note the delight he took in performing chores about the farm. To the boy, already poet, "Fodder-Pullin' Time" was not irksome or laborious, but joyous and satisfying. In the vein of James Whitcomb Riley, humor permeates such stanzas as "Milkin' Time."

As the pages turn, another sort of autobiography is perceptible. Elsewhere, Pearson tells about his first poem, spoken one winter day while riding in a wagon with his father. When asked if he was getting cold, the child intoned,

> *"My fingers and my toes,*
> *My feet and my hands,*
> *Are jist as cold as*
> *You ever seed a man's."*

The little rhyme is not included in this collection, but another is here which he wrote at the age of twelve. It represents the kind of verse a gifted boy would compose when imbued with late Victorian conventions. When he was fifteen, in the last decade of the nineteenth century, his lines move with youthful idealism, then later strike out, as in "To Eugene Debs," with militant vigor. Among the early compositions, Pearson experimented with rhyme and meter. There are, expectedly, gracious echoes of Edgar Allan Poe and, in "Oh, To Be Married in May," a compliment paid John Charles McNeill, the older North Carolinian with whom he shared much. Thus, in the slow, cautious movement towards an attainment of his own unmistakable mature voice, handsomely exemplified in the sonnets, we follow a poetic autobiography almost as engaging as the subjects he treats and the themes he explores.

Throughout the book we are always aware that it is Pearson the Poet who speaks. Supported by a melodiousness and religious fervor which knows its direction, Pearson's philosophy is an optimistic one. If one may not know the future, it is well to fill one's days with work and beauty. While such a stance does not prevent the poet from occasionally being indignant at wasted lives and "proud conceits," he is nevertheless and finally hopeful.

The autobiographical allusions within the poems, and the autobiography of a poet's skill in development, do not, even so, provide the biographical facts. In *Poet's Progress*, thirty-nine chapters of which were published serially in the *Wilkes Record* in 1964-65, Pearson explored the past in order to set the record straight. He was born September 13, 1879, on a lonely mountaintop, Berry's Mountain, five miles from the "Fifty Acres" Farm, in Wilkes County, North Carolina. The cabin was also about five miles from the new campus of Wilkes Community College. It was on the half-way ground between the College and the "Fifty Acres" Farm. Though formal training was sparse in the short-term district schools, he managed to provide himself, whenever he could get books, with an excellent education. Perhaps it was well that there were no teachers to interfere. He announced his ambition in his boyhood: he was going to be a poet. Like Benjamin Franklin and Mark Twain and others in literary history, he went into printing as a first step toward realizing his intention of becoming a writer. By the age of twenty, he was editor of a political weekly in an adjoining mountain county. Eventually he established his own newspapers. Most successful was the *Fool Killer,* a personal journal which brought him considerable fame and money.

The depression years of the 1930s were bleak ones. After the death of his first wife, he remarried and moved down from the mountains into Guilford County. Along with him went his library and a printing press on which he set the type for the last two of five books of his poetry. (All are now collectors' items.) Then days became happier.

On August 4, 1953, at a dignified and impressive ceremony in the State Capitol in Raleigh, Governor William B. Umstead, in accordance with provisions of legislatives statutes, appointed him Poet Laureate of North Carolina, a position he still holds.

Ten years later he returned to his native county to live near his daughter, Mrs. Agnes Eller. There he is to be honored by a special building that is to be built to house his personal library at Wilkes Community College. At the age of ninety-one he is still a very active poet.

This present volume, the most comprehensive to date, contains poems autobiographical in more than one way. It is evidence not only of a life spent in reaching an ambition, but also evidence of the esteem with which he is held among those who love poetry.

Richard Walser

AUTOBIOGRAPHICAL SKETCH OF JAMES LARKIN PEARSON

My father's name was William Thomas Pearson. He was a son of Bartlett Pearson and Dianna (Wright) Pearson. He was born August 7, 1853, and he was only ten years old when his father died in a Yankee prison camp during the Civil War. The home was soon broken up and the boy was an orphan. He lived around among his poor relatives who had more children of their own than they could take care of. He went to school a few weeks now and then in the backwoods school of the neighborhood, but he didn't get much education. In his later life he could read in a slow and hesitating manner, and he could write in a cramped and awkward hand. As soon as he was big enough to be a farm hand he worked around wherever he could get a job. Of course he was never able to accumulate any money. It was just a matter of existing from day to day.

My mother's maiden name was Louise McNeil. She was a daughter of Larkin McNeil and Nellie (Ferguson) McNeil. She was born November 15, 1839. When she was about 15 years old her father was taken down with a severe case of rheumatism or arthritis, so that he became a helpless bed-ridden invalid. It fell to the lot of his daughter Louise to be his nurse and care-taker for TWENTY YEARS. She had got but very little schooling in the local backwoods school. She could read very well if the words were not too hard, but she never learned to write or to read handwriting. She had a regular job of taking care of her helpless father. It was a very confining job and she had no chance to get out among people and get acquainted with young men who might have been interested in her. She knew that all her chances of getting married were slipping away. The years were passing and she was getting to be an Old Maid. But she went on serving in a spirit of love and loyalty, and she taught herself to believe that was the way she was paying for her crown in glory. Louise had an older brother, Frank McNeil, who was a Confederate soldier, and the news came that Frank had been killed in battle some place in Virginia. She had two younger brothers, John and Milt, and they had to shoulder the responsibility of running the little

Beaver Creek farm. In course of time the mother died, partly from heart-break over the war and all the other troubles. Larkin's frail and helpless body clung to life for two or three years longer. Louise was 36 when her father died at the end of twenty years of helpless suffering. Louise was turned loose in the world with no job, no education, and no prospects for the future. All her chances of getting married (if there had ever been any) were gone with the wailing wind. The only thing she could do was to join John and Milt on the farm, trying to make a living.

Nobody now living knows for certain when and how Bill Pearson and Louise McNeil got acquainted. They lived in adjoining neighborhoods and they may have known each other for several years. Or it is easy to guess that John and Milt may have hired Bill to work for them on the farm. It is more than likely that they worked together on the farm. Two lonely people had found some sort of companionship, and as they worked they talked. They talked about the war, the troubles, the living and the dead. And then they talked about themselves. It didn't take them long to decide that they might as well go on working together the rest of their lives. Bill was 24 and Louise was 38. So these two lonely people were married, for better or for worse. They didn't have very much to start with and they knew it would be a hard struggle. Sometimes it was very hard. They started to build a crude log cabin on top of Berry's Mountain. When Bill and Louise got all their possessions in the log cabin they had very little of this world's goods. It was an adventure in faith, and if their faith held out they would get along. They had only four books in the cabin—a cheap Bible, a spelling book, an old school Reader, and an old Baptist hymn book with its covers torn off.

During the early spring-time of 1879 it was discovered that there was going to be another member of the family. Louise, who had been a nurse and later a farm hand, was in a delicate condition and was not able to get out on the mountain farm and help Bill with the crop. It didn't take long to do the small amount of cooking and sewing. So Louise lay down to rest, maybe to sleep a nap. As she woke up her eyes fell on the old hymn book on the table. Why not read the hymns? That would help pass the time. So Louise got in the habit of reading the old hymn-book. Hour after hour she read it. Day after day she read it. She never sang the hymns, but read them in a sort of sing-song manner that was half akin to a tune. Of course Mrs. Bill Pearson, expectant mother, didn't realize that she was doing anything to the little new life that was on the way. Almost certainly she had never heard of such a thing as prenatal influence—how the life and character of an unborn baby may be shaped and influenced by the thoughts and moods of its mother. The spring and summer passed, and soon it was autumn-time. On the 13th of September, 1879, there was excitement in the lonely cabin on Berry's Mountain. The old "granny-woman" was sent for and a big boy baby was announced. That was me. In due time the new baby must have a name. They named me after my great-uncle, James McNeil, and my grandfather, Larkin McNeil. And so, as the fates would have it, I became James Larkin Pearson.

So far as could be discovered by the "granny-woman" and all the visitors, I was a normal baby. They didn't find anything wrong with me. Not then. But about four years later they were not so sure. One cold winter day when I was four-and-a-half years old, my father had me out with him somewhere on the farm. All at once he asked me, "Jimmy, are you cold?" Without taking any time to study out my answer, it came like a flash, and I said:

> *"My fingers and toes,*
> *My feet and my hands,*
> *Are jist as cold*
> *As you ever see'd a man's."*

Back at the house a few minutes later, my father told my mother what I had said, and they were both scared. They were afraid their boy was going to be a poet. No such disease had ever been known in the family on either side, and they didn't know what to do for it. So they just had to wait and watch for further developments. They began to notice that my baby words were often falling into a rhymed and measured pattern. They hoped I would outgrow the disease, but it seems that I never did.

I had already learned my A B C's by looking at the wall-paper on the cabin wall. It wasn't regular store-bought wall paper. It was just any old scraps of newspaper or magazine that they could paste up. One big space on the north wall had been papered with circus posters, with big red and blue letters and pictures of lions, tigers and elephants. I had learned the alphabet from looking at those circus posters. When I was five years old they got me a Webster's Blue-Back Speller and I began learning to spell and read. From very early childhood I had been fascinated by the printed page. I looked at the page of a book and I saw all the little rows of curious marks and dots on it and I wondered what they were. My mother said they were letters and words, and I would have to learn all about them, and then I could read. I asked my mother how the letters and words got put on the paper. She said it was something they called printing, and it was done at a place called a printing office, but she had never seen a printing office, and so she couldn't tell me much about it. But I kept on wondering about the strange thing called printing. How did they get the words printed on the paper? The county-seat town, Wilkesboro, had a printing office and a newspaper, but I had never been to Wilkesboro. Anyway, I kept thinking about it and trying to figure out how printing was done. I reasoned that there had to be something to press down on the paper and leave an impression. Then I supposed that there had to be something like ink on the thing that was pressed down so that some of it would stick to the paper. Nobody had ever mentioned the word "type" to me and I didn't know there was such a word. Then, all at once, I took a notion to make an experiment for myself. I got hold of a piece of thick sole-leather and I took a lead pencil and printed the letters of my name, J. L. PEARSON, on the leather, but printed them backwards or up-side-down. Nobody had told me to do that. I studied it out for myself. Then I took a sharp-pointed knife and began cutting away the leather from around the letters, but leaving the letters standing out. When all the surplus leather was cut away from around the letters of my name, nothing but J. L. PEARSON remained. Then I went down to the back fence where the poke-berry bushes grew and got some of the red berries and made myself some ink. Then I smeared my ink over my leather type and pressed it down on a fly-leaf of my Third Reader. Taking it up, there was my name, J. L. PEARSON, printed as nice as pie. It was the first printing I ever did and the first I ever *saw* done. I still have that Third Reader, and the printing I did that day is just as plain and clear as it was more than 80 years ago. I often show it to my visitors and tell them that I was perhaps the youngest printer in all history. Soon after that, I ordered a rubber type printing outfit from J. Lynn & Company and I was on my way as a printer. I could then print two or three words at a time.

About two years later, when I was ten-and-a-half, I got a chance to go to town, and the first place I wanted to see was the printing office. There I saw a boy running a job press and printing envelope corners. Another boy was picking up little pieces of type metal and standing them in rows. Then over on the other side was the Washington Hand Press where the paper was printed. It had a lever that they pulled, and that made a big heavy thing come down and squeeze the words into the paper. It was the most interesting thing I ever saw, and I knew right then that I was going to be a printer. When I was twenty years old I got a job in another newspaper office and learned to set type, and do all the other things that needed to be done in a country newspaper shop of that period. Two years later I had a small print shop of my own, and I have been connected with the printing business ever since.

But I have run ahead of my story. They didn't start me to school until I was seven, and while I was waiting to be seven I had already got to be such a good reader that the teacher said I didn't need a First Reader and I didn't need a Second Reader. She told my mother to get me a Third Reader—right there in my first year of school when I was seven years old.

My parents were very poor, as already stated. We lived in another log cabin a mile from the school. Often the weather was bad and I couldn't go regularly. We didn't have a school bus to come by and pick me up and take me, warm and dry, to the school house door. I had to walk a mile in the snow or mud. By the time I got to the school house my home-made brogan shoes were so heavy with mud that I could hardly lift my feet. I had to get a stick and scrape the worst of the mud off before I could go into the house. In cold weather the room was heated by a sheet-iron stove, and if you sat close to it you would burn up, and if you sat back away from it you would freeze. The drinking water for the school was brought in a tin bucket from a spring down in the hollow and set on a shelf at the back. It had a rusty tin dipper and everybody drank out of it.

When all my school days were counted up, I hadn't had more than twelve or possibly fifteen months of schooling, all in that one-room free school in the backwoods. We didn't have any grades, but I probably got to what would be the seventh grade. A few of the students were from well-to-do families, and they went on to High School and some of them to College. But I didn't go any further. There was no money, and I was a poor seedy-looking brat from a backwoods cabin and nobody expected me to amount to anything. It didn't matter whether I got an education or not.

But I had become a book-lover and a tireless reader and student at home. I put up a shelf on the cabin wall and started my Library with my three or four school books. Adding to them whenever it was possible, it has taken me more than 80 years to accumulate the 3,000 volumes that make up my present Library.

Just as my parents had suspected when I was four, I became a poet. By the time I was ten or eleven I was writing three or four poems a week. I guess they didn't have a very deep and profound philosophy and I didn't expect them to live forever; but I got a great kick out of writing them, and there was nothing else half so important to me at that time, except printing. Half of my brain was working on poetry and the other half on printing. Of course I was thoroughly committed to the old standard forms and patterns of verse, always expressed in rhyme and meter, and I was anxiously waiting for the day when I could have my own print-shop and print my books of poetry. The time did come when I set myself up as a printer and publisher and I printed and sent out five books of my poems. I was never able to print large editions and give the books a wide circulation. But even the limited publishing that I could do resulted in making my name more widely known than I could ever have expected. Another thing that helped to bring me into prominence about the same time was when I appeared frequently on the Editorial Page of The New York Times. One of the poems that The Times printed was "Fifty Acres," and it was copied and re-copied all over the world. It got me into Who's Who in America for twelve years; and then when I was not publishing anything for awhile the Who's Who people dropped me—thinking, I suppose, that I had passed over Jordan. I never got back into Who's Who in America. But I did get something else that was a big surprise to me. That was in 1953 when North Carolina chose me as its Official Poet Laureate. The North Carolina Literary and Historial Association was responsible for that. Certain members of that organization had been writing letters to the newspapers suggesting that North Carolina should have a Poet Laureate. Several prominent North Carolina poets were suggested as proper candidates, and among them my own name was mentioned a few times. The State Legislature went ahead and passed some sort of a law or ruling giving the Governor authority to appoint a Poet Laureate. But who should he appoint? The Literary and Historical Association appointed a Committee of Nine, and they were scattered all across the State from the mountains to the sea. These nine people, by a secret vote, were to name the person the Governor should appoint. No member of the Committee was to know who the others were voting for. When the votes all went in to Raleigh and were opened and counted—Great Gee-Whilikins! *Every one of them was for James Larkin Pearson.* It was unanimous, and Governor Umstead had no other choice but to appoint James Larkin Pearson as Official Poet Laureate of North Carolina. There was no time limit mentioned and it seemed to be understood that it was a lifetime job. But one bad thing about it was that the Legislature didn't vote me any salary. All the other State officers get a salary, but the Poet Laureate job isn't supposed to be worth anything.

Most of my rich kinfolks turned out to be lawyers, doctors and preachers. But I always said that I couldn't be a lawyer, a doctor or a preacher. Those popular callings didn't appeal to me at all and I had no talent for them. But I did want to be a printer and poet. That must have been the reason I had so much curiosity about the printed page—I was going to write things that would have to be printed, and I had some sort of a prophetic feeling that the two things would go along together in my life. During the years of my childhood and early youth I was just more or less dreaming about what I would do; but when, at the age of 20, I went to work in a newspaper office and was learning how to set type, it seemed that a new world was opening before me. It was a great turning-point in my career and I could begin to see where I was going. It became clear to me then that the print-shop could take the place of the regular school education that I didn't get. A printer has to be careful. His spelling and punctuation must be right, and he must get acquainted with words and how to use them. The print-shop is the ideal substitute for the school room; and so it has turned out that the print-shop has been my school, my university, and whatever education I have today is due in large measure to the fact that I became a country printer. In connection with my writing career, one other thing has become very clear to me: Any young person who has ambitions to be a writer should learn all he can about printing. If he can get a job in a print-shop and stay with it a few years, it will do more for his writing career than anything else can do.

I don't claim to have made any big success as printer and poet, but I have done better with them than I could have done with any other calling. As a lawyer, a doctor or a preacher I would have been a total failure. As a poet, I have written a great deal of stuff that is perishable and soon to be forgotten. But if I have written just one poem that will live, I will go out of this world rejoicing.

I have been married twice, and have outlived both of my wives, and I am coming to the end of my journey without any offspring to follow me. The serious and long-continued illness of my first wife, Cora Wallace Pearson, took care of that. We had one infant daughter who was dead at birth, and there couldn't be anymore. She didn't live long enough for me to get acquainted with her. But we named her Blanche Rose Pearson (which means White Rose) and her name is on the gray granite grave-stone along with Cora's name and mine. Cora died in 1934 and was buried beside Blanche Rose, with a place reserved for me when my time comes. Then my second marriage to Eleanor Fox several years later didn't produce any offspring. My only brother died unmarried and left no descendants. So I am the last of my family line. When I am gone, that will be the end of us.

So, there being no people to go on and represent my family in future generations, I felt impressed with the need to do some-thing about it. I didn't want us to be entirely forgotten. I wanted to leave some mark on the landscape to indicate that we had passed this way. But what could I do? Where was my best chance to get myself and my family remembered? Poetry, of course. If I couldn't do it with poetry I certainly couldn't do it with anything else. There can be different views about which is the highest calling; but there is strong evidence to support the view that when a man or a woman reaches the top in poetry there is no higher place to go. I didn't expect to get to the top nor any-where near the top; but even a modest success in poetry is more enduring than any other thing that a man can do. If he can write just one poem that will live, his name is secure. Several poets could be named who would not have been remembered at all ex-cept for one poem, but that one poem has kept their names alive. I have made a small reputation as a regional poet and I have writ-ten a few poems that have some prospect of living. "Fifty Acres" has already become widely known and has got into sev-eral anthologies. Part of it is in Bartlett's Familiar Quotations. The little Fifty-Acre Home Place three miles west of Moravian Falls is known and read about in many parts of the world.

I am acquainted only with letterpress printing. There is an-other printing process called Offset about which I know very lit-tle; I understand that Offset is developing in three or four differ-ent directions, using photography in many complicated ways. It takes a skill and know-how equal to a university education to be an Offset printer now. So I just let the young men have it and I stay in the old-fashioned letterpress field where I feel very much at home.

In all my 91 years not one drop of intoxicating liquor has ever gone down my throat—unless it was in some doctor's medicine, and I have never taken very much of that. Also, I have never tasted or used tobacco in any shape nor form. Many times I have been with young people who were learning to drink and smoke, and they thought it made them look smart. But I never could have been persuaded to try it.

I have already put up my grave-marker—a large gray granite —at the grave of my wife and baby in the Moravian Falls cemetery. I put Cora's name and the baby's name on the stone, with their dates, and I put my own name with my birthdate and a place for my death-date when that time comes. I also had the engraver put under my name on the stone these three words in smaller letters: PRINTER AND POET. As long as the Moravian Falls cemetery exists those three words will testify to what I wanted to do, to what I honestly tried to do.

Sometimes I am inclined to brag about my good health at 91, and at least I am always thankful for it. But I am fully aware that some day—or some night—my good health will come to an end and they will take me over to the cemetery at Moravian Falls and lay me down beside Cora and the baby, where I will sleep for —nobody knows how long. The Moravian Falls cemetery is a beautiful place to sleep and it is not very far from the mountain-top where I was born 91 years ago. So, after all my restless goings and comings here in this work-a-day world, I will not be very far from home.

Let me say here that I am a religious man—a Christian—in a somewhat unorthodox way. I have an abiding faith in Jesus the Christ as the Savior and Redeemer of the world. But all the fol-de-rol that goes by the name of popular orthodoxy doesn't mean anything to me. Historically speaking, we know very little about Jesus; but those of us who hold Him cherished in our hearts know all that we need to know.

We have always been taught that there will some day be a Resurrection of the dead, but there is wide disagreement about what sort of beings we will be in the next life. One theory is that we will be just disembodied spirits floating around in the air with no feet to walk on, and no head to put our hats on and no tongue to talk with. And yet we are supposed to walk the golden streets and play a golden harp and sing the heavenly anthems through endless eternity. If the Lord wants me to do that, He will have to give me some musical talent and teach me how to sing and play, for I have never been able to do it here. Before the first million years was out, I think I would get tired of toting that golden harp and I would most likely throw it into the first ditch I came to, and I would start looking around for a print-shop where I could set some type. Surely they must have some print-shops in heaven, or else some of us old-time printers are going to be awfully disappointed. When you have worked at a job you love for sixty or seventy years, and then get transferred to a job you never could do for the rest of eternity—it doesn't look like much of a heaven to me.

Another theory is that we are right now almost at the opening days of the Millennium when the devil will be chained and there won't be any more war and sickness and death, and the dead will be raised up and live here as real flesh-and-blood human beings, and the whole earth will be transformed into a beautiful Garden of Eden where corn and beans and potatoes and red, red roses will grow forever in lavish abundance without cultivation and where people will stay young or middle-aged forever and never grow old and die. I do believe that God is able to do that, and if He gets the devil properly hog-tied and put away He might actually do it. I would like that, and I believe I will accept it right now. Amen.

James Larkin Pearson

Memory Bells

BEREFT

In Memory of
Cora Wallace Pearson

They have builded a tomb
In a garden of gloom,
And the flowers that bloom
Have a fainty perfume.

They have shapen a bed
For the beautiful dead,
And a pillow is spread
For the innocent head.

They have buried my queen,
All so white and serene,
And my hunger is keen
For her beauty unseen.

They have lowered the shade
In the room where she stayed,
And we all feel afraid
Of the silence that's made.

3

MY LOVE LIES STILL, LIES SILENT

In Memory of
Cora Wallace Pearson

My love lies still, lies silent;
    She sleeps the longest while.
She does not wake at morning;
    She does not speak nor smile.

Her lips are pale as lilies
    Grown in some shadow'd place,
And something more than beauty
    Lies on her sleeping face.

Her eyes, sealed fast with kisses,
    See not the dark nor dawn,
And from her ears forever
    The sounds of earth are gone.

My love does not remember;
    She does not understand
How long I will be waiting
    In such a lonely land.

I LOVE YOU, DEAR

In Memory of
Eleanor Fox Pearson

"I love you, dear," is such an ancient phrase,
Worn out by jaded lovers long ago,
And we who flourish in these modern days
Should have new words more fitting to bestow
On one whose merits pass all common speech
And dare imagination's boldest flight.
Then let us make improvements till we reach
The perfect utterance of love's delight.

So I bethought me to invent new ways
To try my new premeditated art;
To cover you with passionate high praise
And crown you in the throne-room of my heart.
But my inventions fail and disappear,
And I come back to this: "I love you, dear."

MY BUD AND ME

In Memory of my brother,
John Milton Pearson

My Bud an' me, we raised a calf,
An' claimed it sorter half-an'-half,
Till Paw he give us one, an' we
Then had a calf apiece, you see.
Fust thing we done, right at the start,
We made a little two-wheeled cart.
The wheels wuz sawed off from a tree.
We sawed 'em off, my Bud an' me.

5

Then through each wheel we made a hole,
An' hewed an axle from a pole,
An' split another pole an' sprung
The ends apart an' made a tongue.
We bent some bows an' made a yoke,
An hitched the calves an' got 'em broke,
An' then it was a sight to see
How proud we wuz, my Bud an' me.

My Bud an' me, we went ahead
An' got a box an' made a bed,
An' got some tools an' worked the road
So's we could haul a whoppin' load.
I guess we made a thousand trips
A-haulin' wood an' haulin' chips.
You bet them calves knowed "haw" an' "gee";
We learnt 'em that, my Bud an' me.

I recollect, long time ago,
One winter when thar wuz a snow,
We made a snow-man in the yard,
An' let him freeze till he was hard:
We made his eyes an' mouth an' nose,
An' put him on some ragged clothes;
An' Maw she laughed an' said 'at he
Looked zackly like my Bud an' me.

We uster buy our Sunday suits
By skinnin' bark an' diggin' roots.
We cut the beedwood with an ax
An lugged it home upon our backs,
An' 'round the fire-place after dark
We all set thar a-skinnin' bark;
An' when it dried to some degree,
We sacked it up, my Bud an' me.

6

We hunted beely fur an' nigh,
An' sassafack an' butterfly,
An' it would shore have made you smile
To see us pullin' pennyrile
An' all them things an' many more
We carried to the country store,
An' come back home in highest glee
With things we'd bought, my Bud an' me.

Sometimes when we wuz extra smart
An' sorter got a runnin' start
Ahead of what we had to do,
We'd get to loaf a day or two.
An' then we went an' fished for whales
An' hunted Molly Cottontails
An' had a reg'lar restin' spree
That done us good—my Bud an' me.

We didn't realize it then,
But now that we're old bearded men,
We look back o'er them childish years,
An' sorter brush away the tears,
An' realize the truth at last
That all our happy days are past—
That we no more can happy be
As we wuz then—my Bud an' me.

DUST

Dust is made of fallen trees,
    Stones and blades of grass.
Seasons take their toll of these
    Daily as they pass.

7

Dust is made of bird and beast,
   Weed and flaming rose.
Death, that brings them to her feast,
   No distinction knows.

Dust is made of mighty men
   And their mighty works,
All unmindful where and when
   Dissolution lurks.

Dust is made when beauty dies—
   All her lovely parts—
Women's lips and children's eyes,
   Brides and bleeding hearts.

I have loved so many things—
   Given them my trust.
Oh, but how the memory clings!
   Oh, but they are dust!

JOHN

*John Milton Pearson, the author's only
brother, died April 29, 1923, age 39 years*

In reminiscent mood today
   I turn life's pages o'er,
And pass again the memoried way
   That we have passed before,
And think of how we used to play
   Around the cabin door.

The opening pages of the book
    That memory holds to view
Invite me now to turn and look
    At all the scenes we knew—
The care-free rambles that we took,
    The work we had to do.

When we were little barefoot boys
    A-rolling in the hay,
Or making lots of harmless noise
    With all our childish play,
Life held before us many joys,
    And death was far away.

We went a-swimming in the creek
    When summer skies were blue,
And kept it up from week to week
    The happy summer through.
The glow of health was on the cheek,
    And in the muscles too.

The gay companionship you gave
    Is now forever flown,
And you are resting in the grave,
    Beneath a mossy stone,
And I must suffer and be brave
    And go my way alone.

We sang behind the mule and plow
    When you and I were young;
We dreamed beneath the bending bough
    Where ripening apples hung.
But all the dreams are ended now,
    And all the songs are sung.

MEMORY-BELLS

In Memory of my daughter,
Blanche Rose Pearson

The faint-heard chime of memory-waking bells
  Across dim hills that fade into the past,
Where olden dreams lie buried, and where dwells
  The phantom of the hope that could not last.

So like a silver bell that I have heard,
  Whose echo dwells forever in my brain,
Or like the dreaming note of some rare bird,
  Or like the smell of roses after rain.

Like these, and all sweet things, the thought of one
  Who touched my life a moment and was gone;
But she will rise with some new-waking sun
  And come to me across some silver dawn.

10

Childhood Poems

A RURAL SCENE

The sombre forest, old and still,
　　The hill-range high and wide,
And e'en the merry laughing rill
　　That bubbles from its side.

Still in the orchard trees I hear
　　The brown bees busy hum.
And from the hedge-row standing near
　　The brook's low murmurs come.

Across the wide-spread meadow land
　　The redbird wings his way;
The trees, by vernal zephyrs fanned,
　　Their giant branches sway.

Written at age 12

SPRING

　　The poet's soul
　　Begins to roll
When harsh old Winter closes;
　　When gentle Spring
　　Begins to bring
Her wealth of love and roses.

　　When Cupid flies
　　Beneath the skies
With cherub wings extended;
　　When wind that blows
　　The chilling snows
And wintry days are ended.

When souls sublime
Do swiftly climb
Upon love's mystic ladder;
When every heart
Doth play its part
To make creation gladder.

The blooming earth,
In joyous mirth,
O'er which the sunlight glances,
With hope's own fire
Doth then inspire
The young heart's nimble fancies.

Written at age 13

PICTURES OF A STORM

I see the lightning's vivid flash
That breaks the night asunder;
I hear the curling waters dash,
The burst of booming thunder.

An angry storm-cloud sweeps across
The dark horizon quickly;
The gray old oak trees heave and toss,
With brown leaves falling thickly.

Now through the dark mist of the night
I hear the wild wind wailing,
And in convulsion and affright
The whippoorwills are sailing.

No minstrel ever piped a song
   So full of solemn feeling
As that deep tone which bounds along
   Wide heaven's frescoed ceiling.

The towering hills present a scene
   Disconsolate and dismal;
The murky vales that lie between
   Seem endless and abysmal.

                      Written at age 14

THE APPROACH OF NIGHT

The golden sun is in the west,
Now hanging o'er the mountain's crest,
And soon the world will sink to rest,
Just like a squirrel in its nest.

The evening sky a mirror seems;
It catches all the slanting beams,
And all the many-colored gleams,
And sprinkles them o'er fields and streams.

The shadowy mountain grows more dim;
I scarce can see its ragged rim;
The forest pines, so tall and slim,
Fade out of sight, both trunk and limb.

The day is gone and night is here,
And every object far and near
By slow degrees will disappear,
All swallowed up in darkness drear.

                      Written at age 15

A DREAM OF DELIGHT

When the roses by the river
  To the surface kneel and nod,
Then the merry-hearted plowman,
  And he turns the mellow sod,
Pours his soul all out in music
  Till it echoes up to God—
When the roses by the river
  To the surface kneel and nod.

When the juice is in the melon
  And the melon on the vine,
And the biscuits on the table
  When the farmer goes to dine,
There's a rural invitation
  That the heart cannot decline,
When the juice is in the melon
  And the melon on the vine.

When the bloom is in the meadow
  And the bee is in the bloom,
Stealing sweets from every petal—
  Stealing nectar and perfume—
Then behold the rarest beauty
  That all nature can assume,—
When the bloom is in the meadow
  And the bee is in the bloom.

When the plow is in the furrow
  And the song is in the soul,
And the light of smiling faces
  Fills the earth from pole to pole,
Then we're on our journey homeward,
  And we're sure to reach the goal—
When the plow is in the furrow
  And the song is in the soul.

Written at age 15

16

MY LOVE-SHIP

I launched my little love-ship out
  Upon life's placid sea,
And felt it would, beyond all doubt,
  Bring good gifts home to me.

I waited long for its return,
  Nor spied its silver sail.
My heart did for that love-ship yearn,
  And hope was like to fail.

I dreamed I saw my love-ship fair
  That sailed so far away.
I looked into my heart and there
  It safe at anchor lay.

Oh, there were gifts of rare design,
  And smiles of love and peace,
That brighter o'er my pathway shine
  When other pleasures cease.

That ship now saileth far and wide
  O'er every sleeping sea,
And back across the tranquil tide
  Brings good gifts home to me.

                              Written at age 16

BEAUTIFUL HANDS

Not alone within the mansion
   Where the lords of earth reside—
In the city's broad expansion
   And the gilded halls of pride—
But within the rural cottage
   Where no costly gems abound,
Toiling for their daily pottage,
   Lovely hands are often found.
Beautiful hands are those that do
Deeds of love the whole day through.

Oft the hand by rings encumbered
   Has no charm for bleeding grief,
While the toil-worn hands are numbered
   With the hands that give relief.
Wealth and pride can add no beauty
   To the grasping hand of greed;
But the hand that does its duty
   Shall be counted fair indeed.
Beautiful hands are those that do
Deeds of love the whole day through.

Written at age 16

THANKSGIVING

Let us shout a glad hosanna
   From the green earth to the sky
In thanksgiving for the beauty
   That shall never fade nor die.
Earth is bless'd beyond comparing—
   Let all creatures thankful be
That the valley smiles with plenty
   From the mountain to the sea.

18

There's the plowman with his horses
　　And the angler with his hook,
And the lover with his lassie
　　And the scholar with his book.
Oh, the earth is rolling onward,
　　Leaving sadness in the rear,
And the highway to the kingdom
　　Shines before us bright and clear.

Not a zephyr greets the morning
　　But it bears upon its breast
Incense from affection's altar,
　　Echoes of celestial rest;
And the night of gloom and darkness
　　Is a prelude to the day
That is soon to burst upon us
　　In its golden, glad array.

Then the day will be the brighter
　　For the night that came and went,
And the earth will smile with beauty
　　And the air will breathe content;
And the richest boon of heaven
　　Will upon creation rest,
While the friendship long forgotten
　　Springs anew within the breast.

Thus the Father of the faithful
　　Stretches out His gentle hand
To pronounce the benediction
　　Of His love upon the land;
And the mountains catch the echo
　　And repeat it once again,
And the forest bows approval
　　And vale responds "Amen."

Written at age 17

A LITTLE QUEEN

There's a little fairy queen
    Who is reigning all alone.
She is never heard nor seen,
    Though she's very widely known;
And the realm is all serene
    While she sits upon the throne.

She's so gentle and so sweet
    That her subjects take delight
In their worship at her feet
    From the morning till the night,
And their hearts do proudly beat,
    And their lives are ever bright.

And her kingdom is so wide
    That she knoweth not its bound,
Since that neither end nor side
    Has in any age been found;
And ne'er yet in selfish pride
    Has she on her subjects frowned.

For she guides her Ship of State
    With the helm of faith and trust,
Hence 'tis not her hopeless fate
    On some lone isle to be thrust.
Oh, that queen is good and great,
    And her rulings all are just.

And she grows not old with years,
    Though they number many a score,
For her glad face now appears
    Lovely as in days of yore,
And the people have no fears,
    But they love her more and more.

Through the realm her presence darts
    Swifter than the cooing dove,
And the bliss that it imparts
    Fills all space below, above.
She's the queen of human hearts,
    And her name is simply—Love.

Written at age 18

SONG OF LIFE

Take life—the sad, the pleasing—
    Whatever God hath sent—
The burning and the freezing—
    And therewith be content.

The time for rain or shining
    Is not for you to say;
So therefore quit your pining
    And let life have its way.

If men could rule the weather
    And order bloom or snow,
They all of them together
    Would fill the earth with woe.

They'd find a thousand reasons
    To change creation's plot—
To renovate the seasons
    And make December hot.

Take life—the kind, the cruel—
　　On every side you turn,
And use it all as fuel
　　To make love blaze and burn.

And drop your senseless notion
　　That nature's all mistakes;
For nature brings a lotion
　　For every wound she makes.

Your mission may be humble,
　　Your talents may be few;
Still 'tis not wise to grumble,
　　But simply dare and do.

And learn the truth of living,
　　The secret paths of peace:
Be faithful and forgiving,
　　And from contention cease.

Written at age 18

A VALENTINE

I built a palace long ago,
   With towers passing fair.
I gave it to my love, and so
   She dwells in beauty there.

Upon the north I built a wall—
   A massive wall of stone.
'Tis moss-grown now, and over all
   Full many suns have shone.

Go out, my Valentine, and long
   On tireless pinion soar;
Fly to my love and learn what song
   She singeth evermore.

Go bear to me, like Noah's dove,
   A message from her hand,
Writ in the dialect of love,
   Which all men understand.

Written at age 20

Melody Lane

TROUBADOUR

The world is turning back again
    Along its olden tract again,
And I can see the thousand years
    That crowned the poet's brow,
And I can hear the crooning song
    That led the hungry hearts along—
Along the road to Yesterday
    And back again to Now.

Go deck the town in bunting rare
    And give the streets a gala air;
Bring out the happy-hearted bells
    And ring them up and down.
A messenger from other days has come
    To sing forgotten lays—
A Troubadour, a Troubadour,
    Is passing through the town.

Now we must run to meet the dawn
    Before the night is fairly gone,
And we shall see the Troubadour
    And hear his lute begin;
And he will laugh exceedingly
    And sing his ballads pleadingly
For all the dreaming lady-loves
    That he has come to win.

Oh, he will storm the castle walls
    Till every mossy tower falls,
And he will capture beauty's prize
    And win himself renown;
So let us up and haste away
    To meet him at the break of day—
A Troubadour, a Troubadour,
    Is passing through the town.

CHRISTMAS MORNIN'

Oh, the Christmas dawn's a-breakin'
An' the children are awakin'
An' their little hearts are achin'
    To arise,
An' to know the happy feelin'
That forever comes a-stealin'
Into little hearts a-reelin'
    With surprise.

Although clothin' is a blessin',
They have business that is pressin',
An' they take no time for dressin',
    Like the rest.
Out of bed they come a-hoppin',
With their nighties all a-floppin',
An' they never think of stoppin'
    To be dressed.

To the fire they come a-flockin',
All a-grabbin' an' a-knockin',
To discover what each stockin'
    May reveal.
From the leg a doll is peepin',
With her china eyes a-weepin',
And a Teddy-Bear is sleepin'
    In the heel.

There are candy men a-grinnin',
An' a little top for spinnin',
An' that isn't a beginnin',
    I'll be bound.
Hear the toy guns a-shootin',
An' the bugle-horns a-tootin',
An' the little trains a-scootin'
    All around.

HIS MAJESTY, THE CZAREVITCH

Now the Czar of all the Russians, be it known,
Has at last an heir apparent to the throne,
   And he's sending out his runners
   To inform the naval gunners
That they'll have to run their bloomin' war alone.

Yes, the Czar is in the nursery, mayhap,
With a funny little bundle in his lap;
   And it makes him fairly giggle
   Just to see that youngster wiggle,
And he swears it's just the picture of its pap.

Oh, his cup of bliss is full up to the brim,
And he vows that he is strictly in the swim.
   When he hears that kid a-squalling,
   Trifles like Port Arthur's falling
Haven't any sort of interest for him.

Oh, the Czar has gone to singing "Rock-a-By",
And he's got a happy twinkle in his eye,
   And he doesn't give a kitty
   For the muchly-fallen city,
And as for the dying soldiers—let 'em die.

He has made a "trotty-hossy" of his knee;
He's forgotten that the ships are on the sea.
   Don't disturb his meditations
   With your loud "distress of nations";
He is busy with his baby—let him be.

NEWS FROM THE FRONT

Oh, the men-of-war that ply upon the seas!
Oh, the many aching bosoms, ill-at-ease!
    Oh, the fierce and fearful rattle
    When the navies clash in battle.
Their insatiate thirst for murder to appease!

Oh, the fearless young reporter loves to roam!
He is with them far away upon the foam.
    While the navy men are fighting,
    He is writing, writing, writing—
Making "copy" for the papers back home.

Oh, the telegraph that spans the pulsing earth!
We can never rightly estimate its worth;
    And the cables, oh, the cables!
    How they put to shame the fables
Of the wonders that were never given birth!

Oh, the editors, how rapidly they write!
Oh, the Mergenthalers running day and night!
    And the presses, oh, the presses!
    How they grind out the distresses
Of the great opposing nations in the fight!

MY MOTHER READ A HYMN-BOOK

My mother had a hymn-book, an old-time hymn-book,
    Taken, after battle, from a soldier's breast;
And this she sat a-reading, continually a-reading,
    The summer she was waiting for an unknown guest.

My mother read a hymn-book, a sad-toned hymn-book,
   Read the little verses in a sing-song way,
When I was just a prophecy, a dreamed-of wonder,
   Waiting in the future for a long-sought day.

My mother got the music, the soft, slow music,
   Running like a river in her love-hot veins,
Making every nerve-cell, new growing nerve-cell,
   Answer to the calling of the old sad strains.

So I was set a-singing in an old-time hymn-book,
   Chanting little meters with my unborn tongue;
And always I have listened to the low calling voices
   Of songs that wake within me and must be sung.

TO EUGENE DEBS

Gene, they think that they have covered you with shame,
But they's only crowned and glorified your name—
   Made you kin to Paul and Stephen,
   John of Patmos—Jesus, even—
All the lordly line who've suffered just the same.

Gene, you don't know how you're growing here of late—
How the world is turning now to call you great;
   How your glory-star has risen
   Since they packed you off to prison—
How you shame your persecutors and their hate!

Gene, you only started out ahead of time,
And they thought your shining virtue was a crime;
   But your friends will not forsake you,
   And the world will overtake you,
And acknowledge that your courage is sublime.

Gene, I know it's mighty hard for you to face,
And to spend your precious years in such a place;
    But it's only your refining—
    It will leave you bright and shining—
Standing high among the saviors of the race.

FAR PLACES

The near-by places win me not;
    I think them very cheap.
They have no charm, no magic lure,
    No memories to keep;
For I can go there any day,
    As I have done before,
And see a very common town—
    Just that and nothing more.

But, oh, I'm hungry for the road
    That leads me far away,
To Amsterdam and Edinburgh
    And Tunis and Bombay.
Damascus and Jerusalem
    Are calling me to go.
And Budapest and Wittenburg
    And Rome and Tokyo.

My eager feet would never tire
    Of travelling up and down
To Leningrad and Zanzibar
    And Cairo and Cape Town.
I'm dreaming now of Mandalay,
    And Venice would be grand,
And Copenhagen, Kimberly,
    And golden Samarkand.

But there are folks in every place
    Who long to get away
And make a dreamed-of-pilgrimage
    To this old U. S. A.
The wanderlust is on the hearts
    Of Europe's restless throng,
And they would love to visit us
    And bring their folks along.

Perhaps they think of Raleigh
    When the evening shadows fall,
And Durham, Charlotte, Rockingham,
    And Boone and Rural Hall.
And they would find so many things
    To worship and adore
In Taylorsville and Stony Point
    And Elkin and Lenoir.

HER WONDERFUL EYES

Oh, were I an artist with power to paint
A picture as pure as the soul of a saint—
As strong in conception and rich in design
As the jewels that come from the depth of the mine;
And were I to paint from the coming of spring
Till the swallows go southward on shivering wing,
I never could paint you the picture that lies
'Neath the lovable lids of her wonderful eyes.

If the stars were dissolved and the dews were distilled,
And mixed by a chemist, though never so skilled,
And melted and mixed in the splendid compound;
If the tail of a comet were given me then
To dip and to paint for the children of man,
Though I took for my canvas the scroll of the skies,
I never could paint you her wonderful eyes.

33

Her wonderful eyes! How they sparkle and gleam!
How they mock the outburst of the poet's wild dream!
For they rival the light of the costliest gem,
And her beautiful soul is reflected in them.
I am powerless now that I stand in the way
Where the twibil lights of love cast refulgent their ray.
I am held in the thrall of the power that lies
In the fathomless depth of her wonderful eyes.

THERE IS NEVER ANY CHRISTMAS FOR THE POOR

Oh, they talk about the spirit of the Christ,
    And of how we are to celebrate His birth,
While the poor are being catalogued and priced—
    Being bartered for a certain money's worth.
There are lights along the avenues of gold,
    And the Christmas cheer of opulence is sure;
But the alleys—ah, behold!—
    They are dark and very cold;
    There is never any Christmas for the poor.

When He tramped across the halls of Palestine,
    When He stood among the fishers by the sea,
He was kindred of the human and divine,
    He was brother to the likes of you and me.
But they took Him from the people that He loved,
    And they set Him where the dollar signs allure:
In His name they make a feast—
    They with worldly goods increased—
    But there's never any Christmas for the poor.

Where the festive halls are brightest in their glow;
    Where the music melts and mingles with the air—
There the Christmas congregations come and go,
    And the pick of pride and fashion—they are there.
But if Comrade Christ is somewhere looking on,
    He is saddened by the prospect, I am sure;
And I think His heart must bleed
    For His comrades here in need,
    Where there's never any Christmas for the poor.

EASTER LILIES

Long ago the people perished
    Like the dumb brutes of the field,
And they had no hope of living
    In some heaven unrevealed.
Visions of a resurrection
    Had not dawned upon their view,
And they had no Easter lilies
    Where the deadly nightshade grew.

Like some half-forgotten legend,
    Like some whisper barely heard,
Came the mystic revelation
    Of some ancient prophet's word—
Promise of a coming Saviour
    Who would drive away the gloom
And would plant the Easter lilies
    All around the open tomb.

More and more the light was shining
    As the centuries went by,
And the hearts of men were lifted
    By a faith that mounted high.
Somewhere in the happy future,
    In a land of pure delight,
Surely there would be an Easter,
    And the lilies would be white.

Then at last the Great Fulfillment,
    And the risen Saviour came
With His holy hands uplifted
    In His Holy Father's name.
Suddenly the world was flooded
    With a heavenly perfume,
And the Easter lilies blossomed
    All around the open tomb.

Now there is no stone so heavy
    That it can't be rolled away
In the glad prophetic dawning
    Of the Resurrection Day;
And there is no deadest mortal
    That He cannot bring alive
In the glory of His kingdom
    Where the Easter lilies thrive.

THE LOVE THAT NEVER DIES

Down beside the ancient river
   Where the lofty birches quiver,
And the mellow moon is mirrored
   In the soft translucent wave
There, so silent and so solemn,
   Stands a massive marble column,
And beneath it, flower-laden,
   Lies a lovely little grave.

Undernearth the blushing roses'
   In her purity reposes
One upon whose tender shoulders
   Never sorrow's mantle fell;
But whose sad, untimely going,
   She the truth so little knowing,
In the bosom of another
   Kindled all the flames of hell.

Youth and maiden I have seen them
   With the yard-gate shut between them,
As they lingered in the gloaming
   Ere the parting word was said;
And they used to walk together
   In the early autumn weather,
When the yellow leaves were falling
   From the branches overhead.

In that lonely land where slumber
   Pale companions passing number,
She is still the little maiden,
   Changing not with changing scenes;
But the youth—his brow is wrinkled
   And his hair with white is sprinkled;
You can see that he is ageing
   By the staff on which he leans.

He has lived retired and lonely,
    With no living creature only
His poor dog to share the silence
    Of the long and cruel years;
And he reared the marble column
    Standing there so sad and solemn,
And he planted all the flowers
    And he waters them with tears.

STROLLING IN THE STARLIGHT

Very well do I remember
    'Twas an evening in September,
Such an evening as you fancy
    Might in every way compare
With a clump of ruby roses
    Standing all in perfect poses
In the middle of a desert
    That is desolate and bare.

Now the sun was slowly sinking
    And the day and night were linking—
Marching arm in arm together
    Through the misty mountain wood;
Through the oak-boughs arching o'er us
    Rang the night-bird's nimble chorus,
And the church-bell sent its summons
    To a common brotherhood.

In my soul was something sweeter
    Than all outward earthly meter,
As we marched amid the music
    Of the mountains, you and I,
And the thousand silent voices
    That are heard when earth rejoices,
Wafted to us endless echoes of
    A blessed by-and-by.

Hotel Lithia, calm and queenly,
    On the Brushies sat serenely,
Lifting up her tapered turrets
    Far above the mountain mist;
And the sight grew fainter, fonder,
    As we gazed away off yonder,
Where green verdure clothed the valley
    And the hills were heaven-kissed.

In my bosom darts and dances
    Millions of fantastic fancies
As I hear again the music
    Of the vocal village band;
Then across the dewy heather
    And we mount the steps together,
And we see the village preacher
    As he rises in the stand.

All his face is smoothly shaven,
    And his locks are like the raven;
He is dressed in neat apparel;
    He is handsome, as a whole;
'Tis the Father's gracious greeting
    That the preacher stands repeating:
'Tis a comfort to the conscience
    And a solace to the soul.

'Tis the speaking of the Spirit
    And you hold your breath to hear it,
Until all the earth about you
    Is forgotten for the time—
Until every nerve and sinew
    That is hidden deep within you
Is a-trembling with the power
    Of the language so sublime.

Preaching done, the village pastor
    Prayed the blessings of the Master
On the souls of all the sinners
    Who were looking for the light;
Then, mid people thronging thickly,
    Down the steps we ventured quickly,
From the gaudy glare of lanterns
    To the balmy breath of night.

I am dreaming (Bless the vision!
    'Tis transporting—rapt—Elysian!)—
How I drew you close beside me,
    How I held your little hand;
How my heart would fairly flutter
    With the thoughts it dared not utter,
But I pressed you closer—closer—
    And you seemed to understand.

Ah! That night was truly splendid,
    But alas! Too soon it ended—
Ended in a painful parting
    'Neath the dropping of the dew.
Nothing can its memory smother,
    And I sigh for such another.
May the Lord be pleased to send it,
    And to send me there with you.

On the Farm

THIS LITTLE ROAD LEADS HOME

I know a little crooked road
　　That runs along the ridges,
And dodges in and out among
　　The maples and the pines,
And crosses little singing brooks
　　On little wooden bridges,
And measures off the little miles
　　With little wooden signs.

The little road I have in mind,
　　About which you are reading,
Is not the crowded way
　　That leads into the city's heart;
But out among the farming lands
　　Is where the road is leading,
Where Nature has the upper hand
　　And there's but little Art.

The farm is not commercialized
　　And run for making money,
Where barns are full of blooded stock
　　And tractors pull the plow;
But just a little private home
　　Built where it's warm and sunny,
With garden and potato patch,
　　Some chickens and a cow.

And these remarks are uttered here
　　To call the world's attention
To just a little patch of ground
　　Adjacent to my door;
To show that common little things
　　Are worth a poet's mention,
And full of tender beauty
　　That we never saw before.

A field of corn in summer time
 Can shoot to beat the Germans;
A peach is better than a prayer—
 Or just as good, at least.
A pine can tell me finer tales
 And preach me better sermons
Than ever fell from creeded lips
 Of parson or of priest.

The ants are early out to work,
 For they are good providers
In storing up the scattered wheat
 And other tiny seeds;
And all about the stubble-field
 The small plantation spiders
Have spun their little sailing ships
 Upon their sea of weeds.

September mornings when the dew
 Is heavy on the grasses,
That master alchemist, the sun,
 Turns everything to gold.
The belts of fog along the creek
 Are banked in shining masses,
And of the splendor of the hills
 The half was never told.

The early birds in happy pairs
 Are thick upon the fences,
Or hopping in the faded grass
 To find a bite to eat.
The odor from the fodder field
 Is magic to the senses;
The voices of the calling quail
 Are wonderfully sweet.

I never need to journey
    To the lands beyond the ocean,
Nor yet among the mountains
    And the valleys of the West;
For I have found a little place
    To center my devotion,
And life among my native hills
    Is happiest and best.

FIFTY ACRES

I've never been to London,
    I've never been to Rome,
But on my Fifty Acres
    I travel here at home.

The hill that looks upon me
    Right here where I was born
Shall be my mighty Jungfrau,
    My Alp, my Matterhorn.

A little land of Egypt
    My meadow plot shall be,
With pyramids of hay-stacks
    Along its sheltered lee.

My hundred years of brooklet
    Shall fancy's faith beguile,
And be my Rhine, my Avon,
    My Amazon, my Nile.

My humble bed of roses,
    My honeysuckle hedge,
Will do for all the gardens
    At all the far world's edge.

In June I find the Tropics
    Camped all about the place;
Then white December shows me
    The Arctic's frozen face.

My wood-lot grows an Arden,
    My pond a Caspian Sea;
And so my Fifty Acres
    Is all the world to me.

Here on my Fifty Acres
    I safe at home remain,
And have my own Bermuda,
    My Sicily, my Spain.

HOME PRODUCT

Now these-here poets what we read about—
    What writes all them-thar books—
I've found out somethin' what they ain't found out,
    Er that's the way it looks.

They goes off yander to them furrin lands,
    Them cities 'crost the sea,
An' writes of things nobody understands,
    Especially you an' me.

When, all the time, if they'd jist look around,
    An' had more simple taste,
Jist lots of poem-timber could be found
    That's goin' plum to waste.

Here on the farm an' right around our feet
    Great poems could be found;
An' they'd be purty, too, an' jist as sweet,
    Here on our native ground.

APPLE-TREE SNOW

Upon a breezy day,
About the first of May,
    There was a snow;
And I remember well
How splendidly it fell
    To earth below.

No cloud was in the sky;
No shadow floated by
    With deepening gloom.
I found out my mistake,
And that each snowy flake
    Was apple bloom.

PEACHES

God made the world and set it full
    Of every tree that bloomed and fruited,
And all for man to go and pull
    And taste and try till he was suited.
But there was one that caused the sin
    About which orthodoxy preaches.
I wonder if it could have been
    Peaches?

God practiced on the tangerine,
    The orange, apricot and apple,
And other problems in between
    With which He always had to grapple.
Then being master of His trade—
    A thing that only practice teaches—
God tried His very best and made
    Peaches.

And then God chose the Sunny South
    To grow the best you ever tasted—
The kind that just melt in your mouth,
    And you begrudge the juice that's wasted.
If there's a better land for me,
    Where sin's dark shadow never reaches,
I hope the fruit they have will be
    Peaches.

AN INVALID'S WINDOW

My bed is here by the dingy wall,
And I'm not able to move at all,
And the only world that I can claim
Is just in the shape of a window frame.

My window is open, but all I see
Is a panel of fence and an old dead tree,
And an old cow grazing beside a pond,
And the edge of a corn-field out beyond.

The panel of fence is old and gray,
And covered with vines about half-way.
The old dead tree is a-leanin' some,
And there is a woodchuck—just now come.

The old cow yonder is mostly red,
With a few white places about her head,
And she grazes along from side to side
As if she were very well satisfied.

The pond ain't much in the way of size,
But it's all lit up by the evenin' skies,
And the corn-field fits into place somehow
With the old gray fence and the tree and the cow.

My bed is here by the dingy wall,
And I'm not able to move at all;
But I am happy that I can claim
A world in the shape of a window frame.

FODDER-PULLIN' TIME

My nose sometimes remembers things
    My brain has done forgot.
A happy smell so often brings
My recollection back an' clings
    To some old happy spot.

Of all the good old nature-smells
    That fit into my rhyme,
The one on which my memory dwells
Is that which comes again an' tells
    Of fodder-pullin' time.

When fodder's pulled this mornin' soon
    Its charm is not complete.
About tomorrow afternoon
It's like an old remembered tune
    That time has rendered sweet.

Jes' go out in the evenin' shades
    An' walk between the rows,
An' as you pass the wilted blades
The smell that all the air pervades
    Will satisfy your nose.

Now lookin' back an' thinkin' strong,
    I jes' can't hardly tell;
But if my nose don't lead me wrong,
The thing for which I mostly long
    Is that sweet fodder smell.

LAYIN' OFF

Up dis mawnin' 'way 'fo' day;
Feed ol' Mollie some cawn an' hay;
Eat mah brekfus' an' milk de cow,
An' den hitch up to de shubble plow.

Groun' done broke wid de two-hoss team,
Big plow sunk plum in ter de beam,
An' den drug ober wid section har
Till ain't no clods remainin' dar.

Groun' done meller an' smooth an' sof
An' all jis' ready for layin' off.
De sign o' de moon is a-rollin' around,
An' soon dat cawn mus' be in de groun'.

Done bin out to de timber-track
An' cut some poles an' fetched 'em back,
One eend skun about half-way down,
T'uther een sharp fer to stick in de groun'.

I starts in here whar de field am wide,
An' sets on pole at de yudder side,
Den keeps my eye on de shinin' mark
An' runs dem rows till de fall o' dark.

BILLY'S FARM

There was a young farmer named Billy
Whose farm was a little bit hilly.
   He levelled it down
   And built him a town
And lived him a life that was thrilly.

THE STOOPIN' APPLE TREE

I'm a-settin' here today
In a sort o' lonesome way,
Kind o' dreamin' of the happy, happy time
    When I used to play around
    That delightful spot o' ground
Where the sweet enticin' apples hung in prime.

I was sprightly then an' gay,
Ere my childhood slipped away,
An' my young heart leaped exultant, proud an' free,
    An' my right none dared dispute
    While I picked the lovely fruit
From the branches of the stoopin' apple tree.

In the happy days o' yore
Stood that fruit-tree old and hoar,
Stretchin' out its mossy branches far an' wide;
    An' the little saucy wren
    Lit upon them now and then,
Pourin' forth his notes of praise on every side.

Then the days were bright an' long,
An' my life was like a song,
An' my humble home a palace unto me;
    Then my only wish an' care
    Was to play at leisure there
In the shadder o' the stoopin' apple-tree.

I remember long ago,
When the sun was sinkin' low,
An' the moon began to peep across the hill,
    When the wood was in the shed
    An' the lamp a-burnin' red,
An' the supper bell a-ringin' loud an' shrill.

I remember, when the night
Had expelled the glowin' light,
How I bounded off to bed in childish glee;
How the pictures in the brain
Showed themselves to me again
As I dreamed about the stoopin' apple tree.

But those phantom hopes are flown,
An' my limbs have weary grown,
An' the wild bird's song no longer thrills my breast;
For no more my eyes behold
That delightful place of old,
Where the tenor of the day was gentle rest.

So I picture in my mind
All the words an' actions kind
In a cottage that I never hope to see;
An' the tears o' grievin' rise
In these-here old fadin' eyes,
While I'm thinkin' o' that stoopin' apple tree.

Written at age 17

THE POETRY FER ME

I want some poetry 'at's got
The speckled hen 'at laid an' sot
An' hatched some little biddies out
To run an' foller her about.

The kind o' poetry fer me
Has got to have an apple-tree
All blossomed out with white and pink,
With nectar for the bees to drink.

Some cows must wander through the scene,
A-grazin' where the grass is green,
An' they must also stand an' wait
At milkin' time beside the gate.

A poem never is complete
Without some field o' wavin' wheat,
Some men at work in overalls,
Some rivers an' some waterfalls.

Put in some blue an' tender sky,
An' then some clouds a-sailin' high,
An then, to finish up yer lines,
Put in a patch of old-field pines.

All sich as that is what it takes
To build the kind o' verse 'at makes
The reader clear his throat an' cry,
An' he can't tell exactly why.

EASTER BURIAL

We thought it had been Easter
    And Resurrection Day,
Because the Easter lilies
    Had made a brave display;

Because the early jonquils
    Had come from under ground,
With resurrection glory
    And yellow trumpet sound.

The little tombs of nature
    Were bursting everywhere,
And soon there would be beauty
    A-plenty and to spare.

But wise old Mother Nature,
    So free to change her way,
Called off her resurrection
    And had a burial day.

She brought her robes of ermine
    From where the cold winds blow,
And wrapped the tender flowers
    And buried them in snow.

OLD HOME PLACE

Well, I went upon a journey
    To a place I used to know,
Where we all lived there together
    In the happy long ago—
Paw and Maw and Little Brother,
    And with me we numbered four,
All so happy in the cabin
    On the Yadkin River shore.

So I thought I'd go and find it
    Standing like it used to be,
With its friendly doors open
    And a "welcome home" for me.
But I found the spot deserted
    And the ground was stark and bare.
Only memory existed,
    For the cabin wasn't there.

Paw and Maw and Little Brother
    All were sleeping on the hill,
And there wasn't any "welcome"
    And the place was very still.

So I turned away in sorrow
   From the Yadkin River shore,
Where there used to be a cabin,
   But there isn't any more.

LET'S GO A-FISHIN' ONE MORE TIME

'Long somewhurs in the early teens,
   Ole rush hat on a feller's head;
Ole slick dime in a feller's jeans
   Felt as big as a pone o' bread.
Goin' a-fishin' along the creek,
   Bright June days jist in their prime:
Joy like that I now would seek—
   Let's go a-fishin' one more time.

Seems might 'nigh jist like a dream,
   But I kin tell you the dream was great—
Trottin' along on the bank o' the stream,
   Draggin' the pole an' a-totin' the bait.
Feelin' as rich as a lord, an' then
   Feelin' to see if I'd lost my dime.
Let's be happy like that again—
   Let's go a-fishin' one more time.

Pore ol' back is a-gittin' bent,
   Pore ol' legs is a-failin' fast;
Can't go now at the gait we went
   In them days o' the happy past.
Doggon brain is a-gittin' tired
   Thinkin' o' this ol' foolish rhyme.
Now for the things we've long desired—
   Let's go a-fishin' one more time.

BURNIN' OFF

I say, now, John—and you'll agree—
Fer boys like we-uns used to be,
A heap of pleasure lies concealed
In burnin' off a broomstraw field.

You know that hill at the old Brown place
Whur we played ball an' prison-base
On Sundays with the neighbor boys—
Ah, them-thar days was full o' joys!

Then when the broomstraw yallered good
From all them frosts 'at it had stood,
We longed an' longed like ever'thing
Fer burnin'-off time in the spring.

'Long somewhurs 'twixt sundown an' dark
Paw he would come in an' remark:
"The signs is all perzackly right
Fer burnin' off broomstraw tonight."

Then you an' me most tuck a fit
An' run an' got our torches lit,
An' struck out hard as we could go
Fer that old broomstraw hill, ye know.

We dragged our torches through the straw,
An' kep' right-smart ahead o' Paw.
He follered with a bushy pine
To whup out whur it crossed the line.

Sometimes the blaze was runnin' high
An' lightin' up the earth an' sky;
Then dreckly it would change about
An' jis' come purt-nigh goin' out.

Sometimes, too, when the wind was still,
The fire went creepin' up the hill;
The long straws burnt off at the ground
An' fell like dead men all around.

I use-ter watch 'em doin' that,
An' thought 'bout whur the war was at:
The straws was soljers that-a-way,
That fell an' died, an' thar they lay.

An' somethin' else I liked so well
Was that-thar-pleasant smoky smell
That jis' kep' lingerin' about
Long after all the fire was out.

It's funny how a feller's nose
Will recollect sich smells as those,
Recallin' things we heard an' saw
When we was kids a-burnin' straw.

THE FLOWER CATALOGS

The flower catalogs are here,
    And that's a sign of spring.
In colored covers they appear
From busy seedsmen far and near,
And though it's early in the year,
    It's quite the proper thing.

I love to turn the glossy leaves
    And see the colored plates;
My breast with satisfaction heaves
At seeing how the artist weaves
His fancy colors in his sheaves
    Of gardens and of gates.

57

The leafy lanes as pictured there
　　Invite my willing feet,
And I would like to wander where
The pictured paths are green and fair,
Pervaded by the perfect air
　　Of some serene retreat.

I want to buy some seeds this spring,
　　And lay me out some bowers,
And all else to the four winds fling,
And many loads of richness bring,
And never do another thing
　　But piddle with the flowers.

IN THE FALL

In the fall the shocks of fodder
　　Stand in long and perfect rows,
And the leaves are turning crimson
　　Where the friendly forest grows.
Mountains look far off and smoky
　　And the sky is lost in haze,
And the air has got the odor
　　Of the sad autumnal days.

In the fall the frosty mornings
　　Make us build a bigger fire,
And we want an extra blanket
　　When at evening we retire.
In the fall the hungry possum
　　Climbs the tall persimmon tree,
And the possum dog is waiting
　　When he comes down, don't you see?

58

In the fall the lusty pumpkin
Smiles in grandeur to the skies,
Then there is the smell of baking,
And you love those pumpkin pies.
In the fall the sorghum boiling
Brings a time of perfect bliss,
And the famous autumn poet
Turns out poetry like this.

THE LITTLE MOUNTAIN

It ain't so much, as mountains go.
If just a mountain's all you seek;
For others make a bigger show—
For instance, there is Mitchell's Peak.

It ain't well known like Pilot Knob,
Nor famous like old Rondyvoo;
But it's a purty decent job,
A-standin' up there bold an' true.

When we lived there at the McNeil Place,
The Little Mountain was enough,
With Yadkin flowin' at its base,
An' Stoneman's Road around the bluff.

Though ages pass, I'll not forget
Them Easter Sundays, long gone now,
When all us jolly youngsters met
An' climbed the Little Mountain's brow.

The gals, a never-endin' charm,
  Feigned weariness with feeble groans,
An' then we took 'em by the arm
An' helped 'em o'er the rugged stones.

Them picnic baskets, rounded high,
   That we took with us on the climb!
The good fried chicken, cake an' pie—
   I'd love to taste 'em one more time.

At last, upon the mountain peak,
   We stood an' looked far down below,
An' trained our wonderin' eyes to seek
   The far-off panoramic show.

The farms an' pasture lands we knew—
   Our own dear cottage with the rest—
Lay spread before us like a view
   From some sweet region of the blest.

Away to eastward, through the haze,
   Wilkesboro was sleepin' in the sun,
Across the river met our gaze
   A new metropolis begun.

A telescope we always took;
   It fetched the far-off places near;
An' everybody had to look,
   An', oh, what wonders did appear!

If heaven would, in course of time,
   Grant me one joy to hold in store,
I'd like to go back there an' climb
   The Little Mountain one more time.

ANDY GOULDS'S MILL

My Maw she said the meal was out—
    Thar weren't another dust.
She couldn't bake no supper bread,
    With brown an' crunchy crust.

My Paw he shelled a turn o' corn
    An' poured it in a sack,
An' off to Andy Goulds's mill
    He lugged it on his back.

I toted jist a little turn,
    Bekaze I was so small,
An' brother John weren't big enough
    To tote no turn at all.

But he just went along with us,
    As little fellers will,
To cross the river in the boat
    At Andy Goulds's mill.

Jim Lane, the dusty miller-man,
    With corn-meal on his coat,
Come down an' "sot us over"
    In the little leaky boat.

We watched him as he poured the corn
    'Way up thar in a box,
An' watched it come a-dribblin' down
    Between the grindin' rocks.

The water-wheel it screaked an' groaned,
    As 'round an' round it went;
The rushin' water foamed an' splashed
    In restless discontent.

Jim Lane, the patient miller-man,
    His clothes all dusty-white,
Stood thar a-feelin' of the meal
    To see if it was right.

Paw sot down on a wooden box
    An' watched the spoutin' meal,
While me an' John, we kep' our eyes
    Upon the turnin' wheel.

Back home at last, the three of us,
    Had all had such a thrill,
A-goin' with our turns of corn
    To Andy Goulds's mill.

Then Maw she put the skillet on,
    As all good bakers must,
And then she baked some supper bread
    With brown an' crunchy crust.

ODE TO THE PEACH BLOSSOM

Peach blossom! Peach blossom! Oh, what is your hurry?
    I fear you are coming too soon.
I fear you'll get bitten in April's cold flurry—
    You'd better have waited till June.

You're not well informed in regard to our weather,
    Or you wouldn't dare to come out.
It never is nice more than two weeks together
    While winter keeps hanging about.

You're thinking, no doubt, it's the middle of summer,
    And you're away yonder behind;
But to tell you the truth, you're a premature comer,
    And soon you'll be changing your mind.

THE OLD MAN'S OPINION

You may talk about your palace
    And your splendid city halls,
And the carriage that conveys you
    To the banquets and the balls;
But you're talking mighty simple
    When you undertake to tell
That the country ain't a fitten place
    For decent folks to dwell.

Tell me truly, city neighbor,
    Don't you think you'd like to be
Out among the hills and valleys
    Where the cows roam fat and free,
With the breezes all about you
    And the sunshine overhead,
And the bees-a-sucking honey
    From the blossoms white and red?

Why, you'll never taste the pleasures
    That are showered down to men
If you don't come out among us
    And forsake your drowsy den.
You should see the light spray dashing
    Where the mountain torrent rolls,
And you'd feel a great deal better
    If you'd sun your sleepy souls.

WHEN CAPTAIN LINDSAY FERGUSON
WAS HANDIN' OUT THE MAIL

When Captain Lindsay Ferguson
    Was handin' out the mail,
An' rootin' for the moral code
    An' makin' it prevail,
It was the joy of our lives
    To "order off" for things,
An' get our little packages
    And cut the wrappin' strings.

An' when we ordered story books,
    All full of love an' hate,
He told us we should hurry home
    An' chuck 'em in the grate.
We hurried home, I will admit,
    As fast as we could trot;
But did we burn the story books?
    Well, no sir, we did not.

We hid 'em in the old bed tick—
    Away down in the straw—
Jis' like they was "forbidden fruit"
    An' plum aginst the law.
An' then we managed to escape
    Our mother's watchful eye,
An' sot up late, defyin' fate,
    An' read 'em on the sly.

Thar was our J. Lynn Catalog—
    Our very dearest friend—
A-waitin' till we had a dime
    Or quarter we could spend.

Each time we got a package
    From the famous J. Lynn store,
We found inside an order blank
    So we could order more.

We took that J. Lynn Catalog,
    An' took our pen an' ink,
An' labored with that order blank
    An' didn't sleep a wink
Till we had made our order out
    For two-bits worth of joy;
An' if you do not understand,
    You haven't been a boy.

'Twas not the money value
    Of the stuff that J. Lynn sold,
For brass was more than diamond-dust
    And tin was more than gold.
J. Lynn possessed a magic
    That was never known to fail
When Captain Lindsay Ferguson
    Was handin' out the mail.

THE RABBIT'S NEST

The rabbit's nest is in the straw
    Beneath that bushy little pine—
The cutest nest you ever saw—
    And he is sleeping warm and fine.

The wind is blowing from the west;
    The skies are gray and overcast,
And all around the rabbit's nest
    The snow is falling thick and fast.

But every little snow flake
    That falls upon the bending limb
Will bend it lower still and make
    A warm and cozy house for him.

The cold will never reach him there;
    The wind will pass above his head;
And, oh, how "comfy" he will fare,
    Asleep there in his winter bed!

Sacred Moments

AN INWARD PRAYER

We are hungry for the bread
    That will satisfy the soul;
We are longing to be led
    Where the living waters roll.

We are begging for the balm
    That will heal the broken heart,
And we seek an inward calm
    That will nevermore depart.

We are weary of the road
    That our bleeding feet have trod;
We would take up our abode
    In the palaces of God.

Father, keep us in Thy care,
    Lead us in Thy holy way;
Save us from the tempter's snare
    For Thy mercy's sake, we pray.

We are weak and we are blind,
    Darkly groping after Thee;
Maker of the finite mind,
    Lift the veil and let us see.

Let us, weaklings that we are,
    Take to us the better part;
Let us view Thee from afar,
    Pure and perfect as Thou art.

We have followed frantic men
    Through a legion empty creeds;
We have worshiped them, and then
    We have shuddered at their deeds.

We have been full often cast
    Helpless on confusion's sea;
We have come to know at last
    There is nothing true but Thee.

Take us to Thy Father-Heart,
    Tender Shepherd of the sheep.
From the cruel world apart,
    Let us on Thy bosom sleep.

THANKS

For love that holds our human ranks
    United in an equal bond
    That looks the silent grave beyond,
Accept, dear Lord, our humble thanks.

For all the mercy we have met,
    And all the passion we have slain;
    For all the good we hope to gain
Beyond the silence of regret.

For strength in every time of need
    To stand securely and to trust,
    As all Thy chosen people must,
And follow where Thy footsteps lead

For sun and shower ever blent
    To crown our labors with success;
    And we would thank Thee none the less
For all the trials Thou hast sent.

For these, and all good things beside,
    We come to render thanks today—
    We come to thank Thee and to pray
Thy peace among us to abide.

SINGING ON THE WAY

The Lord who came and died for us
Will certainly provide for us,
    And in that home
    Where angels roam
Have crowns all laid aside for us.

Those angel bands will sing to us,
The bells of heaven ring to us,
    And all the bliss
    That here we miss,
That happy time will bring to us.

This life's a rugged way for us,
But there's a better day for us;
    So as we plod
    Along to God,
We hope you all will pray for us.

WHEN THE EARTH WILL BE A PARADISE AGAIN

It was once upon a day,
In the ages far away,
When our father Adam lived in Eden's bowers,
    That the Eden fields so fair
    Lay around him everywhere,
And no troubled thoughts disturbed his happy hours.

That was Paradise indeed,
And there wasn't any need
For the doctor and the undertaker then;
    And I'm happy in the thought
    That redemption has been bought,
And the earth will be a Paradise again.

It was just the serpent's lie
That has doomed us all to die—
That has filled the whole creation with the curse;
That has led us on parade
Through the Valley of the Shade,
To the sad and solemn rumble of the hearse.

But our Lord has paid the debt,
And we'll have our Eden yet,
When He comes to bring salvation unto men;
So I'm singing on the way
While I'm waiting for the day
When the earth will be a Paradise again.

A SONG OF TRUST

From God to earth the blessings fall;
    From earth to God our thanks arise.
We cannot know His ways withal,
    We only know that He is wise.

We lay our lives down at His feet,
    A simple, trusting brotherhood;
And all our days are calm and sweet,
    Because we know that He is good.

We are as children when they feel
    A father's hand upon their heads;
And gladly in the light we kneel—
    The light His smiling favor sheds.

We lay us down at close of day
    Beneath the shade of angel wings,
To hear angelic fingers play
    Upon a harp of golden strings.

THE COMPASSIONATE CHRIST

O patient Man of Sorrows,
   O Lamb without a spot,
From whom the churchman borrows
   A name he merits not:
Dear hands uplifted, bleeding;
Dear lips in mercy pleading;
Dear feet to heaven leading—
   How soon have men forgot!

How great Thy loving-kindness
   To all the human race!
But men in mortal blindness
   Have mocked Thee to Thy face.
They take Thy name, but follow
Where empty form rings hollow,
And vain ambitions swallow
   Their heritage of grace.

A HYMN OF THANKSGIVING

Our Father, by whose guardian hand
   Thy little ones are kept and fed,
And by whom, in this desert land,
   For us an ample feast is spread.

Forgive the weak, the faithless heart,
   The failing trust, the broken vow;
Bid all our questionings depart,
   And let us trust Thee, even now.

For Thy dear love that faileth not
    To point us to the heavenly way;
For all that crowns our earthly lot,
    Accept the homage that we pay.

Accept the broken song we raise
    Before Thee in this holy hour,
And all the remnant of our days
    Protect us with Thine arm of power.

THE INNER SIGHT

The town, the village and the farm,
    Aforetime all so commonplace,
    Have robed themselves in richer grace
And don'd a more enduring charm.

The things wherein I only saw
    The base, the brutish and the wrong
    Are rich in themes of holy song,
And loyal to the perfect law.

I cannot walk the meadow path
    And not behold a smile of God,
    Whereas, when first the path I trod,
I only saw His frown of wrath.

And hence it is that I believe
    We find the thing we truly seek,
    Though be it strength when we are weak,
Or be it comfort when we grieve.

KITE-STRING

A boy one day was flying his kite,
And it went so high it was out of sight,
And I said, "O boy with the wind-blown hair,
How do you know there's a kite up there?"

The boy pulled on the string and grinned,
As he looked far into the tugging wind,
And he said, "O sir, it's an easy thing,
For I feel its pull on the tightened string."

A man one day, when the troubles came,
Was heard to call on the Holy Name,
And I said to the man bowed down in prayer,
"How do you know there's a God up there?"

The man looked at me in calm surprise,
And there was love in his trusting eyes,
And he said, "O sir, when my heart is full
Of the love of God, I can feel His pull."

WHO ENTERS HEAVEN

Who enters heaven by the door
    Shall find himself a guest,
And he shall thence depart no more,
    But share its endless rest.

Who climbs to heaven by the wall
    And breaks in like a thief,
Shall soon be broken by his fall,
    And perish in his grief.

PROPHECY

The word of the Lord, by the mouth of the prophet,
    Descended and came to the people and said,
In the beauty and strength and simplicity of it,
    "Ye all are My family; I am the Head.

"Go fell me the trees of the forest primeval,
    And build Me a temple all steady and strong,
And shake the old earth with a mighty upheaval
    Of worship and blessing and music and song.

"Go into the horrible slums of the city
    And bring out the poor and the sick and the lame,
And feed them and clothe them and show them your pity,
    And teach them to honor My beautiful name.

"And so shall your days be as rivers of water
    That flow through a land of perpetual spring;
And ye shall escape from the places of slaughter,
    And rest evermore at the feet of the King."

THE MAGI AND THE STAR

Across Judean hills afar
There flamed a Star,
And Wise Men, tented on the plain,
Went forth amain.

Arabia, Egypt and the East,
On chosen beast,
Fared forth upon their sacred quest
At God's behest.

Day after day, night after night,
The Star gave light,
And went before and guided them
To Bethlehem.

Then straight into the ox's shed
The men were led,
And from the manger looked and smiled
The promised Child.

And lo! The bearded prophet men
Were happy then,
And bowed the reverent knee in prayer
And worshiped there.

REFUGE

In the day of His wrath,
    When He shakes every nation,
May we walk in the path
    That leads on to salvation.

In a dark world of hate
    We are pilgrims and strangers,
And surrounded by great
    Tribulations and dangers.

When the heavens shall fall
    And the earth rend with curses,
We'll escape from it all
    By His infinite mercies.

THE TREE THAT GREW A CROSS

I

That holy night when Jesus lay
    A manger-child in Bethlehem,
A bursting acorn rent the clay
    Hill-high above Jerusalem.

No angel came from heaven's throne
    To celebrate its natal morn;
But, unannounced and all unknown,
    A broken-hearted tree was born.

A little oak began to grow
    Out there upon the wooded hill,
With some unhappy gift to know
    The mission that it must fulfill.

So growing, there the tree had stood
    For more than thirty fateful years,
While Jesus grew from infanthood,
    A man of sorrows and of tears.

II

The Christ went out upon the hill—
    The dear Good Lord went out to pray—
And all the trees were very still
    To hear the words that He would say.

As near the trees His footsteps fell,
    They all rejoiced in trunk and limb,
And in soft whispers tried to tell
    Their all-abounding love for Him.

But one poor tree among the rest
    Stood bow'd, ashamed and trembling there,
And moaned as one who is oppressed
    With sorrows terrible to bear.

"Why art thou sad, O sister tree?"
    The others cried with leafy hum.
"Thou art as strong and fair as we,
    "And, lo, the Christ, the Christ has come."

The sad tree wept its bitter loss,
    And mournfully it made reply,
"I grow the timbers of a cross
    On which the Lord must bleed and die."

SMALL-TOWN NEWS

Great Nineveh had given birth
To mighty kings to rule the earth—
To Nimrod, Sargon—men of might—
And dancing queens for her delight.
    But Nineveh was not the town
    Where God's new glory would come down.

Proud Babylon had mothered sons
Who grew to be her mighty ones—
Nebuchadnezzar, king and beast,
And young Belshazzar at his feast.
    But Babylon was full of sin,
    And God's son could not enter in.

Eternal Rome, in pomp and state,
Sat pondering that she was great,
And boasting of her royal fame,
And all the Caesars she could claim.
    But wicked Rome was not the place
    Where God would show His shining face.

Small Bethlehem was just a town—
A village street of no renown;
But it was near to heaven's heart,
Divinely blessed and set apart;
　　And there, upon a Christmas Morn,
　　The King of Glory would be born.

ISRAEL

A song, O Israel, for thee,
　　Thou wonder of the ages,
Whose fadeless blood all men may see
　　On history's red pages.

Thy destiny was written large
　　In God's first dream of nations,
And there He gave His angels charge
　　Concerning all thy stations.

From being led of God secure
　　Through all the unknown dangers,
Ye listened to ambition's lure
　　And served the gods of strangers.

And then upon thy truant eyes
　　There fell an awful blindness,
So that ye failed to recognize
　　God's greatest deed of kindness.

Because of Judah's slaughtered Lamb
　　Thy Highest hopes were shattered,
And thou, the seed of Abraham,
　　Through all creation scattered.

Oh, sadder than all tragic tales
    That touch our hearts to pity,
Arose thy never-ending wails
    For thy lost Holy City.

For every land hath been to thee
    Gethsemane's sad garden
And many a red Golgotha tree
    Hath pleaded for thy pardon.

But now, forgetting all the past,
    Its age-long tragic story,
Thou shalt be gathered home at last
    In all thy former glory.

For Judah's sun is in the east,
    And Israel's dawn is breaking;
The night of wandering is past,
    And Zion's hope is waking.

When broke is the oppressor's rod,
    And all thy wrongs adjusted,
Thou wilt not doubt the living God
    In whom thy fathers trusted.

Thou who hast borne the exile's brand
    Through ages of oppression,
Behold today thy Promised Land,
    Thy dearly-bought possession.

Now let thy hand reach out and take
    Thy harp from off the willow;
No more the thorn thy bed shall make,
    No more the stone thy pillow.

But pleasant paths in valley's sweet,
 By Zion's living waters,
Shall bless at last the bleeding feet
 Of Israel's wandering daughters.

Say not thy hopes are burned away
 To silent dying embers:
Lift up thy smiling face and say,
 "God lives and still remembers."

WORSHIP

A little rough cabin of poles
 Alone in a region remote;
But now in the hut that the forest enfolds
There gathers a group of devotional souls,
And deep through the mountain the melody rolls
 From many a musical throat.

A simple but tender appeal
 Goes up on the pinions of prayer;
And while at the altar they reverently kneel,
Their hearts overflowing with spiritual zeal,
Each hearer is made to instinctively feel
 That truly 'tis good to be there.

Then slowly, again and again,
 The preacher reads over his text;
It gives us a glimpse of the Evergreen Plain
Where harmony, beauty and holiness reign;
It comes as a heavenly lotion for pain
 To hearts that are troubled and vex'd.

O LORD, THY WORLD!

O Lord, Thy world is reeling
  From self-inflicted blows.
Benumbed and dull of feeling,
  It staggers as it goes.
It needs Thy touch of healing
  To end its present woes.

O Lord, Thy world is broken
  Upon the rack of pain,
And tears and fears betoken
  That every hope is vain.
But if Thy word be spoken,
  Eternal peace shall reign.

THE LITTLE KING OF PEACE

It was a little thing, they said—
  A thing that they would scorn.
Why notice, in an ox's shed,
  A helpless infant born?
They knew not, having souls so dead,
  That it was Christmas Morn.

The great ones, with their blinded eyes,
  Had seen no shining star;
Had heard no music in the skies,
  Through heaven's gates ajar,
Nor knew that holy men and wise
  Had journeyed from afar.

Alas, for all the mighty kings
    That strut upon the earth!
For they shall be but broken things,
    And things of little worth;
And all because an angel sings
    About a Baby's birth.

Today, in time of strife and fear,
    With all the world aflame,
We feel His presence very near,
    And lift our eyes and claim
Our dearest privilege—to hear
    That little Baby's name.

The name of Jesus—evermore
    'Twill make earth's joy increase,
When from the agonies of war
    The nations find release,
And swap the kings of battle for
    The little King of Peace.

High Adventure

LINDBERGH, COLUMBUS OF THE AIR

The following poem was written to mark the 10th Anniversary of Lindbergh's famous flight to Paris on May 20, 1927, and it was entered in a Lindbergh Poetry Contest that I didn't win. But, anyway, I thought the poem was good enough to keep.

The old, old tales have ever and again
    Across our world uncertain shadows cast
Of gods and deities and mighty men
    From some forgotten past.

The Grecian gods, forth faring from the skies,
    Drew down to earth the undreamed eager hour
When men might pale with thunders of surprise
    And miracles of power.

In days that followed, when the Greeks no more
    Provided gods of high heroic size,
The gods of Rome grew powerful and bore
    The banners of the skies.

And then we heard, from many a prophet's lip,
    That all the heathen gods were dead and done,
And their dead souls had manned a phantom ship
    Sailing against the sun.

But as the old gods go, new gods arrive;
    Time pays in kind for all she takes away;
And Hector's courage, Jason's dream, survive
    In men that live today.

Romance still lives, and Mystery invites,
    And men have yet such splendid things to dare;
And who is this that leaps the heaven-heights,
    Columbus of the air?

Who is this casual youth to kingdom come,
    Who writes indelibly his deathless name
Across the heavens, to a motor's hum,
    In characters of flame

One in whose heart the fabled heroes live,
    Who feeds on miracles as daily bread,
Stood forth to prove—and had the proof to give—
    That wonders are not dead.

To take the mad Atlantic to his breast
    And tame it like the taming of a pet;
To marry in a day the East and West
    That never erst had met;

To telescope the ends of Time and Space,
    And pack Eternity into a day;
To put the Furies in a servant's place
    And make the winds obey;

To write new meaning into heaven's scroll
    And give to poetry an epic theme—
This was the brave conception of his soul,
    And this his splendid dream.

The white-hot fire of inspiration burned,
    A fervent torch to light his trackless path,
As if Saint Joan's spirit had returned
    To dare creation's wrath.

He knew what terrors lurked in every mile
    Of that great leap that never had been made,
But courted death and danger with a smile
    And would not be afraid.

His eagle courage threw a bridge before
  The flying rapture of his airy steed—
A bridge of living faith that held and bore
  The burden of his need.

No thing of steel and canvas, no dead weight
  Of bare mechanics clave the startled air;
But somehow—more inscrutable than fate—
  Invention's soul was there.

'Twas no mere man that sat those grilling hours,
  Nerve-taut and eager, driving through the skies;
It was humanity's collective powers
  That looked from Lindbergh's eyes.

Before the flyer's face, as on he sped,
  Old Neptune tumbled from his wave-built throne;
Demons of danger scurried far ahead
  And Lindbergh sailed alone.

Alone was he, and yet companioned well—
  The Spirit of Saint Louis was his mate.
Together they would challenge deepest hell
  Or hold a tilt with fate.

The Spirit of Saint Louis was alive—
  A winged nag, a Pegasus indeed—
And thrilled her poet rider with the drive
  And glory of her speed.

Topping the world's Parnassus at a leap,
  He joyed to feel her muscles flex and strain;
Her nostrils wide, her hot lungs breathing deep,
  His hand upon her mane.

He urged her on; caressingly his voice
  Spoke tender words of courage in her ear;
And she would know, and she too would rejoice,
  When victory was near.

And victory came. On him, a youth unknown,
  And on the plane that carried him so well,
Such sudden light as beats upon a throne
  In floods of glory fell.

They tried to spoil him with unseemly praise;
  They tried to buy him for their vain delight;
But his clean modesty in all his ways
  Was greater than his flight.

Unspoiled by all the clamor of the globe,
  Unbought by all the offers of reward,
He wrapped his glory round him as a robe
  And wore it like a lord.

Old endless Time will tax her every art
  To tell how Lindbergh, child of humble birth,
Flew like a poem to the open heart
  Of all the shouting earth.

DEATH FOUNDERED

One sat at meat whose garment was a shroud,
Eternally erect and pale and proud;
  Her pleasant wine was all men's mingled blood,
And at her feet the dying world was bowed.

The naked bones of all the human race
Were heaped about her in that awful place;
  But the raw taste of all devoured flesh
Filled not the hungry hollows of her face.

90

Her gourmand appetite was like the sea
That never fills, though all the rivers be
    Poured out forever in its open lap,
And all the floods of heaven are set free.

Her name was DEATH that sat before the feast,
And in her mouth the greatest and the least
    Go one appointed way that turneth not
Till all appointed years of men have ceased.

Her eyes reach out and follow every birth
That gives a living creature to the earth,
    And never may it wander from her sight
Till she have tasted what its life is worth.

So sat she through the wilderness of years,
The queen of sorrow and the bride of tears,
    Devouring greedily all fruits of life,
And laughing grimly at men's mortal fears.

Till I beheld and saw upon a day,
The jaws of DEATH set motionless as clay;
    The hands of DEATH lay folded in her lap,
And all the red, ripe flesh was pushed away.

When I would know the cause of such a case,
There came a look of wonder to her face,
    And pointing over Europe, she replied:
"Behold the shambles of the human race!"

Then lurching back into her sunken seat,
As one who must acknowledge her defeat,
    In wailing tones she cried, "Oh, I am sick!
Bring hence no more at all for me to eat."

"Because the soul within me groweth faint
With too much flesh of sinner and of saint,
  And, seeing how they gorge me more and more,
I, patient DEATH, do utter my complaint.

"For have I not been faithful to my trust
In turning all things back to mother dust?
  What waiting wage have I refused to pay
Of all men's hidden sin or lying lust?

"The old sweet sins that have men in control,
That steadily exact their steady toll,
  Till pain be shapen as a knife that cleaves
The broken body from the dying soul.

"I called alike the humble and the great,
And none of these prevailed with me to wait;
  But all the bones of them from day to day
Were picked and piled together on my plate.

"Disease, and accident, and feeble age,
And all the wars that men knew how to wage—
  All these could scarcely furnish me enough
To satisfy my hunger's cruel rage.

"But out of Germany these latter years
A blood-red devil on the earth appears
  Whose cruelty is so much worse than mine
That I am sick and melted down with tears.

"This devil, claiming partnership with God,
And smiting many nations with his rod,
  Has made a butcher-yard of all the earth,
And built a tomb to cover every clod.

"It is too much. I cannot go the gait.
My stomach has been turned by Hitler's hate.
  Another corpse I hope to never see.
Close up the feast and take away my plate."

THE VALLEY OF TEARS

Once, when the world was folden
   Heavy with unshed night,
Hidden and unbeholden
   Of God's piercing sight,
Thou didst awaken and borrow
   Time from the unborn years,
Sorrowful mother of sorrow,
   O Valley of Tears.

Thy unmade hills were shaken,
   Thou yet-unbuilded earth,
And brooding space was taken
   With pains of cosmic birth—
With pains that went before thee,
   Abreast with nameless fears,
When laboring nature bore thee,
   O Valley of Tears.

Slow as the feet of the ages
   Treading the grapes of wrath;
Having such wine for wages
   As no mortal hath;
Born of such bitter crying
   As no mortal hears,
Thou camest, doomed and dying,
   O Valley of Tears.

Then we, like insects breeding
   Within some stagnant fen,
Came forth of thy blind leading,
   A blinder race of men—
Of men whose voice of wailing
   Is loud in heaven's ears,
But barren and unavailing,
   O Valley of Tears.

Nursed at the breast of passion,
    Rocked in the cradle of pain;
Eating, with lips turned ashen,
    All things bitter and vain:
Here where no star hath risen,
    Here where no light appears,
Faint we in thy dark prison,
    O Valley of Tears.

THE TRAGEDY OF A SOUL

Once a soul, forlorn, forsake,
    Trembled into space;
By dread shadows overtaken,
Ushered hence, with reason shaken,
Where no summer mourns awaken,
    And no day of grace.

Through Death's valley, unattended,
    Went that weary soul—
Devious darksome courses wended;
Into unknown depths descended,
Where King Death, with Darkness blended,
    Ever hath control.

Out of time, no map nor measure
    Creeping aeons know.
Onward with a deadly leisure,
Dumb alike to pain and pleasure,
Hoarding up their ghastly treasure
    Of unuttered woe.

Dark, with only fitful flashes
    Of a demon's eye,
Looking out from matted lashes
O'er a barren world of ashes
Sifted from untimely crashes
    'Twixt the earth and sky.

'Reft of every hope and driven
    From the universe;
Crimson-stained and unforgiven,
That poor soul hath madly striven
Till the walls of night are riven
    With an endless curse.

Angels, from their heavenly towers,
    Looking out, can tell,
By the sparks in upward showers,
And the laugh of Evil Powers,
That another victim cowers
    At the mouth of hell.

LOST WORLD

Old world, you're moving mighty fast;
    I wonder what such hurry means,
And what will be the end at last
    Of all your money and machines.

Perhaps you think the trip is hard.
    (And it is hard enough indeed);
But you had best be on your guard
    Against so great excess of speed.

95

The end is not so far away,
    Nor yet so much to be desired,
That you should hasten on the day
    And get there desperately tired.

'Tis true there may be hills to climb;
    'Tis true the going may be rough;
But you'll do well to take your time,
    Because you'll get there soon enough.

When I was young and full of pep,
    I tried to go your breathless gait;
But now I'm tired of keeping step,
    And I would rather stop and wait.

A man who's lost in woods at night
    And cannot judge by sight or sound,
Will never get directions right,
    But always travels 'round and 'round.

Old world, you're like that hapless wight—
    With all your chattels and your goods,
You've missed the highway in the night—
    You're lost and rambling in the woods.

In this your race with life and death,
    You're running on a circle track;
I have a mind to save my breath
    By waiting here till you get back.

THE LAW OF SEX

In the dawn of the first great Epoch,
    Ere the sun was a swirl of mist,
Ere the earth was a dream in God's great scheme,
    Two vertices met and kissed.

96

And there on a bed of chaos,
    Too happy to hide their shame,
They slept till the morn when Sex was born
    In a burst of cosmic flame.

Then out through the empty spaces
    Where matter had never been,
God looked and saw the expanding Law,
    And under the Law was Sin.

From center to far-off center
    There hurried a quickening pull:
Each nebulous core grew more and more
    Till the empty space was full.

The love of the moon for its mother,
    And the love of the earth for the sun,
And the sun's hot chase for a point in space
    Where the strong love-currents run.

The love of the steel for the magnet,
    And the love of the moth for the flame;
Electricity's fire making love to the wire—
    These loves are all the same.

The love of a man for a woman,
    The love of the star for the sky—
There is just one call that explains it all—
    There is just one reason why.

From the greatest of suns and systems
    To the microscopic specks,
They are feeling the draw of the one great Law—
    The immutable Law of Sex.

EARTH BOUND

I was there as a rimless cypher
    When Time had not begun,
A part of the primal Nothing—
    The Nothing that was not made.
Before the dream of the world was,
    And before the birth of the sun,
I slept in the friendly Darkness,
    And never was I afraid.

I was nothing at all but Nothing,
    With neither body nor soul;
With never a thought nor feeling,
    With never a joy nor pain
I had no use for an Ego,
    And sought not any goal—
Had nothing to lose forever,
    And nothing at all to gain.

But somehow, strangely, slowly,
    Through ages that dawned and died,
Hot worlds took shape and motion
    As the miracle winds grew rife.
With a dim, dumb urge of Being
    That never would be denied,
I was swept from the old dead Chaos
    On the billowing tides of Life.

So I found myself one morning
    Awake in a world made fair
With all the bewitching beauties
    That Deity could contrive;
And when I had got acquainted
    And tasted the bracing air,
I was reconciled to the newness
    And happy to be alive.

I don't know where I came from,
　　And I don't know where I'll go;
It all looks dark behind me,
　　And a little bit dim ahead.
This may not be the best world—
　　It's the only one I know;
I wasn't cut out for a nomad,
　　And moving is what I dread.

I'm kith and kin to the mountains;
　　I'm brother to every hill;
The valleys are all my sisters
　　In beautiful robes of green.
I'm cousin to every river
　　That turns an ancient mill,
And brother-in-law to the brooklet
　　O'er which the daisies lean.

I'm here, at least for the present,
　　And satisfied to stay,
But willing to move on further
　　If a better place is found;
And I wonder if up in heaven
　　They'll have some new-mown hay,
Some hedges of honeysuckle,
　　And robins hopping around?

I'm on my way to the World's End.
　　And the road would lead me straight,
But it's all the same in the long run
　　If I get there late or soon;
And so I take to the by-ways,
　　And I linger and loaf and wait;
I stop to look at the new grass
　　And wonder about the moon.

THE FLIER

Remember, if you can,
His day of birth,
And how they said a man
Had come to earth.
A native of the soil,
And minus wings;
Fore-doomed to work and toil
With earthly things,

Along earth's common way
He came and went;
His feet on solid clay,
And well content.
Of manly labor fond,
He did not ask
For anything beyond
His daily task.

From some uncharted shore
Outside of space,
There passed a dream before
His lifted face.
No vision of the night
That slumber brings,
But sudden gift of flight—
A dream of wings.

Now floats above the cloud
A huge machine,
And gravity has bowed
To gasoline.
From old earth-limits free,
And set afloat,
He sails the upper sea
Like any boat.

His old earth-centered eyes,
His wingless mind,
Re-focused for the skies,
New visions find.
The shapes of earth grow dim,
And fade from view.
The only road for him
The pathless blue.

The earth becomes a toy
Hunt out in space,
Where he may run with joy
His airy race;
Proclaiming as he runs,
"Farewell to sod!"
Companion of the suns,
And son of God.

Humor and Dialect

MILKIN' TIME

Once, upon a mornin' dreary,
When I went to milk Old Cherry,
With my basket full o' nubbins
    An' my bucket on my arm,
I was free from all suspicion
That the blamed old brute was wishin'
For a chance to kick me nearly
    All the way across the farm.

So I stroked her hair so silkin,
And sot down and went to milkin'
Just as I had been a-doin'
    Ever since the Civil War.
Then she turned her head an' shuck it,
An' I nearly drapped the bucket,
But I couldn't quite discover
    What she ever done it for.

One more pull at Cherry's faucet,
Where a briar had raked across it,
And there seemed to be an earthquake
    Like the late one in Japan.
Milk was pourin' down my collar,
An' I hadn't time to holler
Till the earth flew up an' hit me,
    Quite contrary to my plan.

Coat-tails flew an' buckets clattered,
But the only thing that mattered
Was my go-to-meetin' breeches
    Ripped from Abraham to Ike;
An' my Sunday hat was flatter
Than a cake of buckwheat batter
An' I tried to sort my bruises,
    But they all felt just alike.

Now I'm feelin' very bitter
Toward that old ungainly critter,
An' I'd rather live on Postum
    Than to milk her any more;
An' I'd surely love to sell her
To some brave an' fearless feller
Who has got the nerve to milk her,
    Even when her tit is sore.

LOT'S WIFE

The Old Man Lot had a house and lot
    On Sodom's Great White Way;
He paid no rent; he was content;
    But he wasn't allowed to stay.
Old Sodom town must be burned down,
    For that was God's decree;
And God told Lot that he must trot,
    And he mustn't look back to see.

"Take child and wife and run for life,
    To save your family's blood;
For I'll rain down upon that town
    A fire-and-brimstone flood."
Then Old Man Lot, he tarried not,
    But made great haste to flee;
And as he fled, looked straight ahead,
    And he didn't look back to see.

But Mistress Lot, it seems, was not
    As good as her old man;
So as she fled she turned her head,
    And looked back as she ran.
Her race was o'er—she moved no more;
    She was no longer free:
With sudden halt she turned to salt
    When she looked back to see.

But all the rest right onward pressed,
    Obeying God's command;
With firm intent their thoughts were bent
    On reaching a safer land.
No backward glance, by any chance,
    To tell them what might be;
'Twas all her fault she turned to salt,
    And they didn't look back to see.

The Old Man Lot and his daughters got
    To a cave in the mountain wall;
But the lady fair, she was not there,
    And she never did come at all.
It was her fault she turned to salt;
    But here's what puzzles me:
How did they know that it was so
    If they didn't look back to see?

ADAM AND EVE

Once the cooties got on Adam,
Though he didn't know he had 'em,
And he said to Eve, "O Madam,
   I'm a-feelin' mighty quare.
There is somethin' in my dressin'
That is terribly distressin',
An' I'm openly confessin'
   That it's more than I can bear."

Eve said, "Adam, I was hopin',
When with you I went elopin,'
That you'd never take to dopin'
   Nor to drinkin' ruddy wine.
But I see you've been a-boozin'
Till your reason you're a-loosin'.
Oh, I did some sorry choosin';
   I'm ashamed that you are mine."

Adam said, "I'm not a-drinkin',
As you seem to be a-thinkin',
An' there's been no glass a-clinkin'
   Underneath my Roman nose.
Stop your base insinuatin'
An' begin investigatin'
To discover what old Satan
   Has been puttin' in my clothes."

Eve said, "Adam, go to strippin';
Peel yer shirt an' shed yer hippin' "—
"If you hadn't eat that pippin,"
   Said old Adam to his mate,
"We'd have had no nasty garments,
Catchin' dirt an' breedin' varments,
An' nobody preachin' sarmunts
   All about our fallen state."

"There you go," said Eve, a-grinnin',
"Blamin' me with all the sinnin';
Don't I spin an' weave the linen
    That conceals your ugly frame?
If I'd left that apple stickin'
When I saw it needed pickin',
You'd be feathered like a chicken,
    An' you'd say I was to blame."

Adam said—no, I'm mistaken;
For his faith in words was shaken,
And he felt himself forsaken,
    And his speech of no avail.
So he hushed an' went to clawin'
Where he felt them lice a-knawin'.
Now it's time for my withdrawin',
    And so ends this tragic tale.

GOIN' AWAY

I'm goin' away on the evenin' train—
    Goin' to be gone for a right-smart spell;
Looks sorter cloudy an' looks like rain—
    Guess I better take my umberell.

Wind's from the north an' it may turn cold,
    An' I've got a ticklin' in my throat;
Wouldn't get sick for a bag of gold—
    Guess I better take my overcoat.

When I get out to Sam's and Jane's,
    I know their table will be a treat;
But there ain't no certainty in them trains—
    Guess I better take me a bite to eat.

Always get dirty on that-thar ride,
　　Though I can't tell as it ever hurts;
But just for the sake of a little pride,
　　Guess I better take me a change of shirts.

Might get asked to a brilliant ball
　　Where I could dance with a painted beaut.
Now what if I was to?　Hang it all,
　　Guess I better take my evenin' suit.

If I'm goin' out for a high old time—
　　If I'm goin' to go the pace that kills—
I just won't look at a measly dime—
　　Guess I better take me a roll of bills.

Might meet up with a robber band,
　　As wealthy travellers often do;
So, in order to stand my hand,
　　Guess I better take my forty-two.

Say, this old suitcase ain't no good—
　　Ain't a-goin' to hold all this-here junk.
Done crammed in just all I could—
　　Guess I better take my biggest trunk.

I'd hate like thunder to get most there,
　　An' then think o' somethin' that I'd forgot;
So, in order to keep my business square,
　　Guess I better take my house an' lot.

Aw, plague the luck!　I just declare
　　It's too much trouble to run about;
An' I ain't got the time to spare—
　　Guess I better give my journey out.

A MILLION OR TWO

I wouldn't be rich if I knew that I could,
For wealth is a burden and not any good.
My tastes are all simple, my wants are but few,
And I could make out with a million or two.

Just a plain little shack built of marble or stone,
And a little more swell than my neighbors can own,
With a few thousand books that I'd never read through,
And that wouldn't cost but a million or two.

A few dozen servants to come at my call;
Some jewels, and pictures, and music, and all,
And three or four cars that are shiny and new—
Why, it all could be had for a million or two.

You see, I'm a man with a moderate taste,
And I don't care a snap about money to waste;
And I'll state as my private and personal view
That a man doesn't need but a million or two.

If Ford were to offer to give me his pile,
I'd wave it away with a satisfied smile,
I'd thank him profusely, but swear it was true
That I didn't want but a million or two.

I wouldn't be rich, for I never could see
That riches would add any honor to me.
Such honor as that I shall never pursue,
But I *would* like to have just a million or two.

GINGERSNAP

Seen old Gingersnap today—
    Fust time since I sold 'im.
'fected me in sich a way,
    Had to go an' hold 'im
By his bridle, careless-like,
    Pet his nose an' praise 'im;
Talk up to'im big as Ike—
    Like I didn't raise 'im.

Standin' thar a-lookin' so
    Lonesome-like an' dreamy:
Perked his years an' whinnied low—
    Awful glad to see me.
Ast him, in a gineral way,
    How he's bin a-farin'.
Looks like he's bin gittin' hay
    Jis' a leetle sparin'.

Could a-cried if any need—
    Wasn't half a-tryin'.
Didn't want that noble steed
    Catchin' me a-cryin'.
Tuck my old bandanner out,
    Blowed my nose a little;
Then cut off a simern sprout
    An' begun to whittle

Seein' that old crackerjack
    Sorter unexpected,
Sot my mind a-runnin' back,
    An' I rickollected
All them days that uster be
    When we worked together,
Doin' farm-work, him an' me,
    In all sorts o' weather.

112

Plowed the ground fer sowin' wheat;
    Later turned the stubble;
Had some fun 'twas hard to beat,
    Well as lots o' trouble.
Couldn't "track" the crooked furs;
    Collar wouldn't fit 'im;
Tail got full o' cuckleburrs;
    Gnats an' hoss-flies bit 'im.

Them days wasn't much, somehow,
    While they was a-goin';
But to look back at 'em now
    Makes a better showin'.
Call back twenty years or so—
    Never mind the weather!
Put us out thar in the row—
    Me an' him together.

TO OUR EVOLUTIONARY ANCESTORS

O man—O monkey—tadpole—protoplasm—
    What e'er thou wert from which we evoluted—
To thee I now address this rhymed spasm
    On questions long disputed.

I know not if thou hadst two legs or forty,
    If thou didst walk or fly or go a-swimmin',
Or if thy skin was hairy, thick or warty,
    Or like us men and women.

I know not if thy home was in the ocean,
    Or high amid the forest boughs a-swinging;
Or if thy young was tended with devotion,
    And motherhood's soft singing.

113

But that's all right—I guess thou wert as happy
    As we, thy children here where time hath thrown us.
How dost thou feel to be our race's pappy?
    Art thou ashamed to own us?

GROWING OLD

I used to get up bright an' early,
While dewdrops on the grass were pearly.
Almost before the break of dawn
I'd be out mowin' on the lawn.

Or else, to show my hardihood,
I'd cut a cord or two of wood,
Then run some errands for my wife,
To show that I was full of life.

I used to walk erect an' proud,
The admiration of the crowd;
Breathe deep to exercise my lung,
An' keep myself a-lookin' young.

But that was in another age,
Before the wars began to rage—
Before this great "preparedness" drive
To conscript men of sixty-five.

Now all at once I find it pays
To do some changin' of my ways.
I lie in bed and grunt and groan,
Almost as helpless as a stone.

An' when I do get out of bed,
I look like I am nearly dead.
Now all my joints are full of pain,
An' I can't walk without a cane.

I'm goin' to let my whiskers grow,
An' paint 'em white as drifted snow,
An' keep some linament in store
To rub my joints when they are sore.

I'll get so blind that I can't see
To tell a hay-stack from a tree,
An' get so deaf that when folks shout,
I don't know what it's all about.

My cravin' to be young an' spry
I now declare to be a lie.
While this big war-scare keeps alive,
I want to look like ninety-five.

HAVIN' FUN

A boy must have a dog an' gun
An' be out some-whurs on the run,
An' that's what he calls havin' fun.
Or else he wants a hook an' line,
An' his old gang that he can jine
Along the creek whur fishin's fine.

An' after fishin' has been tried,
Jis' strip off naked to the hide
An' swim across to t'uther side.
An' then swim back—kersplash!—kerspat!
To whur he left his britches at—
Thar ain't no fun to equal that.

A boy ain't got no time to spend
A-talkin' to some passin' friend
'Bout when the times is goin' to mend.
The only thing that bothers him
Is when the eatin' 's sorter slim,
Or Maw she tans him with a limb.

Of course he ain't no bloomin' saint,
But what's the difference if he ain't?
Jis' let him wear his circus paint;
Bekaze, when all is said an' done;
A boy jis' ain't a-livin' none
Unless he's havin' lots of fun.

SPARKIN'

Reckon you heard about Mandy?—
    She's got married at last;
An' her ol' man is a dandy—
    Seventy-five or a-past.

Funny the way they courted—
    Started along last fall.
Commonly been reported
    She done it nearly all.

Him a-settin' an' chawin'
    An' spittin into the fire.
Her a-hunchin' an' drawin'
    Her chair a little bit nigher.

Her a-pettin' an' scholdin'
    An' a-tryin' to make him hear.
Him a-gruntin' an' holdin'
    His hand behind his ear.

But never mind the **sparkin'**,
　　No matter how it looked.
As I was just remarkin',
　　She's got the old man hooked.

THE BABY

This is the way the baby looked
　　Fust time ever I seen its face—
Lyin' there with its fingers crooked
　　Over a ruffle of baby lace.
Smilin', it was, in its baby way,
　　Movin' its lips with a suckin' sound;
Never a-havin' a word to say;
　　Turnin' its head an' a-lookin' around.

Wonderin', maybe, about the earth—
　　Bangin'est world it ever saw.
Two days out from the date of birth,
　　Fully persuaded the deal was raw.
Wonderin', too, at the awful way
　　Grown folks butcher the English tongue—
(Oogle and google and ta-ta-ta)
　　When they're a-talkin' to one so young.

Pore little baby has kicked an' cried,
　　Tryin' to make folks understand.
None of its needs have been supplied,
　　Nobody gives it a helpin' hand.
Seein' at last what fools they be—
　　Nobody havin' the sense of sheep—
All tired out to the last degree,
　　Pore little baby has gone to sleep.

'RITHMETIC

If I tell you my trouble,
  And you tell me your'n;
Then both will be double
  And cannot be borne.

But you tell me your pleasure
  And I'll tell you mine;
Then we'll have double measure,
  And that'll be fine.

THE POLITICIAN'S CHOICE

The local politician
  Ain't runnin' any more.
He's simply gone a-fishin'—
  A-loafin' 'long the shore.

He don't attend the speakin'
  To hear the boys shout;
He's on the bank a-seekin'
  To catch the frisky trout.

And when election's over
  And all the countin' done,
The candidate's in clover—
  Because he didn't run.

CONSOLATION

Run mighty hard for office,
　　An' didn't git nary smell;
(But Liza Jane, she made a crap,
　　An' we're doin' pretty well).

Rid all around the country,
　　An' spoke most every day;
(But my little gal, Maud Muller,
　　She kep' on a-rakin' hay).

It's hard on the pore man, brother,
　　When the office passes by;
(But Bill an' Tom, they kotch a coon,
　　An' I guess we're a-livin' high).

I AIN'T NO CANDIDATE

I couldn't hold no office job
　　Ner run no government;
I couldn't face the frownin' mob
　　Ner quell the discontent.

I couldn't mount no cracker-box
　　An' wave my arms an' yell,
An' say the country's on the rocks
　　An' goin' plum to hell.

I ain't no hand at slappin' backs
　　Ner tellin' campaign jokes,
Ner puttin' on no phony acts
　　To fool the common folks.

I ain't got no ambitious plans
    To be somebody great,
With lots of business on my hands,
    An' big affairs of state.

GOT ME BEAT

The mocking-bird is in the tree
A-singin' little songs to me,
While I sit here beneath the limb
A-writin' little poems to him.
He just don't seem to have no trouble
In makin' his throat trill an' bubble.
The melody that he's a-droppin'
Don't never show no signs o' stoppin'.

But these-here poems, you can bet,
Are hard to do an' make me sweat.
They make me hollow-eyed an' lean
To get them out of my old bean.
So I just guess that I had better
Knock off an' write a business letter.
He has to such perfection risen,
He'll sing my songs as well as his'n.

A SPRING SPASM

The Easter hats have blossomed,
    Spring dresses have come in,
And the crop of politicians
    Is big enough to thin.

Old cow has gone to shedding,
  Calf's old enough to wean,
And over on the mountain side
  The trees are getting green.

The folks are planting 'taters
  And tommy-toes and peas,
And the smell of fertilizer
  Is wafted on the breeze.

"Spring fever" is sure to get you,
  But when you don't feel right,
A pint of home-made bitters
  Will mend you up a sight.

I dread the cold in winter;
  In summer I dread the heat;
But dog my cats, beloved,
  If spring ain't hard to beat.

A NIGHT IN JUNE

The June-bug roosted under a leaf,
  And the fire-fly winked at the cricket;
The bullfrog sang from the lily-pond
  To the owl in the ivy thicket.

The old mule switched his bushy tail,
  Now free from the tiresome crupper;
The toad licked out his long red tongue
  And caught him a fly for supper.

The whippoorwills met in the twilight air
  And there held a conference, maybe;
The old cow stood by the pasture fence
  And low'd to her bovine baby.

The house-dog howled at the rising moon
  By simply the force of habit;
The fox crawled through the old brush fence
  And raised his hat to the rabbit.

THE HORNET'S NEST

I finded me a hornet's nest
  A-hangin' from a rafter,
An' I decided that was jest
  The thing that I was after.

I runned and gotted me a stick
  An' gived it several punches,
An' them-thar hornets purty quick
  Jist covered me in bunches.

Gee-whillikins! I runned to Maw,
  A-knockin' an' a-yellin',
An' I jist bet you never saw
  A swell'der case of swellin'.

HOT AND COLD

A day in June—and it was hot—
    About as hot as I have felt;
And even when the sun had sot,
    It seemed to me that I would melt.

There wasn't any breeze at all
    To lend a bracer to the air,
And every bug that tried to crawl
    Was panting like a hunted hare.

And then when sleepy time arriv—
    The proper time to go to bed—
You don't know how much I'd have give
    For some cool place to lay my head.

I opened all the winders wide
    And skinned off nearly all my clothes,
And flung the sheets and things aside
    And lay down there on top to doze.

I guess I must have gone to sleep,
    Because I didn't wake no more
Till day was just about to peep
    And the old clock was striking four.

I made a pass at that-thar sheet
    And tore it open with my toes,
And I wish I may never eat
    If I weren't doggon nearly froze.

YOU JIS' AS WELL LAUGH AS TO CRY

Yes, honey, I know it's a tough old world—
    I've tried it a right smart whet.
Been joggin' along the best I could,
    An' I ain't got nowhere yet.
But, say! I've studied me out a plan
    That I sorter wish you'd try:
Let in an' smile fer a little while—
    You jis' as well laugh as to cry.

Yes, honey, I know how bad it hurts
    To be on the losin' side,
To trudge your weary way on foot
    While thieves an' rascals ride.
There's always somethin' to hold you back,
    An' you can't tell hardly why;
But a great long face won't win the race—
    You jis' as well laugh as to cry.

Yes, honey, I know that you an' me,
    If we could have our way,
Would like to reform the human race
    An' hasten a better day.
But jis' because the job's too big
    An' the victory nowhere nigh,
There ain't no call to set an' bawl—
    You jis' as well laugh as to cry.

Shoals and Shallows

THE PRICE OF VICTORY

Oh, smile and be cheerful no matter how fearful
    The long odds against you in life's bitter race.
The more you must master of pain and disaster,
    The greater your joy in the conqueror's place.

Success, when arriving with too little striving,
    Is never secure in the go-lucky hand.
The chances are many that every poor penny
    Will run through the fingers like hour-glass sand.

But sweat down a collar in earning each dollar,
    And you will appreciate how it was got.
The chance happy-landing is not in good standing,
    And waiting for windfalls isn't so hot.

There isn't much glory in telling the story
    Of one to whom Fortune just handed her pile.
We like it much better to see the go-getter
    Who stays in the race till the very last mile.

THE RURAL PHILOSOPHER

Yes, pard, this-here life we're a-livin'
    Is a tiresome old business at best,
An' we ain't none of us a-gittin'
    No extra allowance of rest.
We've allers been mighty dependent,
    An' I rekon we allers 'll be,
An' fer my part, I ain't a-lookin'
    Fer no fortune to settle on me.

We can't all accumulate millions
   No matter how hard we may strive;
Fer ten men will end up in failure
   Where one man'll hang on an' thrive.
It's jist in the nature of people
   In different positions to dwell;
But I guess, old part, on an average,
   We're gittin' on tolerably well.

At least, I am not a-complainin'
   Of nothin' that happens along,
But I jist take life as I find it,
   An' sweeten its cares with a song.
You'll find it is better to whistle,
   No matter how gloomy you feel,
An' a jolly good laugh is a tonic—
   It's mighty-nigh good as a meal.

THE SECRET OF ATTAINMENT

When the clouds are all about you
   And you get to feeling blue,
And you come to the conclusion
   That nobody cares for you
That's the time that you should rally
   All the courage that you can,
And determine, with God helping,
   That you mean to be a man.

Take an interest in living,
    Champion a worthy cause,
And content yourself with little
    In the way of man's applause;
Then you won't be disappointed
    If you fail to get a raise,
And your joy will be the greater
    When you strike a job that pays.

Always look upon your failures
    With an optimistic eye;
If you'll only keep a-going
    You will get there by-and-by;
And at last when you are standing
    On Attainment's sunny brow,
You will feel like smiling—
    Smiling at the things that grieve you now.

There has never been a voyage
    But a little gale has blown,
And there is no path of roses
    That will lead you to a throne;
So, my worthy friend, believe me,
    It is much the wiser plan
Just to pull yourself together
    And move onward like a man.

PUTTING THE QUESTION

It was on the broad Atlantic,
    And the storm was at its height;
All the passengers were frantic—
    Nearly paralyzed with fright.

But the Captain loved the ocean,
    And he said, in passing by,
"All in favor of this motion
    Make it known by saying 'I'."

I WANT TO BE LAZY AWHILE

I've been mighty smart this summer;
    I've plowed and I've hoed my crop;
An' I ain't even laid in the oak tree's shade
    To take me a noon-time nap.
But now the summer is ended,
    And the work's all finished in style;
So my physical force has changed its course,
    And I want to be lazy awhile.

All summer I kept my courage
    Keyed up to the highest note,
In the daily stew of the work to do,
    And the burdens I had to tote.
But now the leaves are falling
    And drifting into a pile,
And I want to let loose from the things of use,
    And I want to be lazy awhile.

I want to get out in the open,
    Like a fairy or an elf,
With nothing to do for a month or two
    But just enjoy myself,
And sleep—by Ned—if I want to—
    Yes, sleep with a peaceful smile.
Send Duty away till another day,
    And let me be lazy awhile.

GRIEF AND GLADNESS

Some lives are clad in mourning
   And grieve themselves away
If one brief night approaches
   To mar their constant day,

While other lives are thankful
   To see one gleam of light
Break through the dark horizon
   Of their cold, cheerless night.

THE MAN WITH THE BROKEN PROMISE

I walked the political highway,
   Which is much crowded now,
And I found, by the wayside fallen,
   A man with a broken vow.
I healed his wounds and set him
   Once more in the walks of men;
But the man with the broken promise
   Never runs as well again.

The man who has lied to the people
   Will long receive their frown,
Although he strives to do better,
   And to live his record down.
He may live for years thereafter
   And be true with tongue and pen;
But the man with the broken promise
   Never runs as well again.

AND THIS IS FATE

One man is born to dominate
And be the master of his fate,
While ten are born to trembling stand
And beg for favors from his hand.

The one is born with mental wings
To soar above the common things;
The other ten cannot advance
Beyond the wall of circumstance.

VIEWPOINTS

I

The world is dark and gloomy,
　　The day is sad and long;
And folks are hateful to me,
　　And everything is wrong.
For, oh, my love is yellow;
　　She broke my heart today.
She passed with some new fellow
And looked the other way.

II

The world is bright and beamy
　　From morning until night,
And folks are glad to see me,
　　And everything is right.
The fashions are such witches—
　　I needn't have been blue.
It was a girl in britches,
　　And, oh, my love is true.

132

AN EMPTY BOAT

Broken and bruised on many a cruel bar,
Over dark waters far,
Hither alone in midnight cast afloat,
Drifteth an empty boat.

Slowly the waves retire, the storm has ceased,
And from the waking east
Dawn's radiant finger, poised in ambient air,
Points to the wreckage there.

An empty boat and one poor broken oar
Cast out upon the shore:
Answer, oh, wandering winds of the hungry sea:
Where may the boatman be?

THE POLITICIAN

Oh, the mighty politician—
   He is with us once again,
With his heaven-ordered mission
   In behalf of mortal men.

He will spin you in his motor
   For a dozen miles or more,
Though you're just a common voter
   That he never saw before.

He can straddle all the fences
   On a hundred-acre farm,
And befuddle all your senses
   When he takes you by the arm.

First he pats you on the shoulder,
    And he whispers in your ear;
Then he gets a little bolder
    And he sheds a little tear.

Time goes on, and he's elected,
    Then upon his office door
Words like these may be expected:
    "I don't know you any more."

GOOD ADVICE

I've given lots of good advice,
And had it followed once or twice;
And folks that want advice from me
Can always get it—and it's free.

I know the how and why and which
About this thing of getting rich;
But giving my advice away
Just keeps me poor from day to day.

NO ESCAPE

If we might go away
Just for an idle day,
In pleasant ways to roam,
And leave ourselves at home!

The thing that bores us so
When off to play we go—
The thing that seems so wrong—
We take ourselves along.

TENEMENT

From window to window,
    Across the way,
A clothesline struggles
    To catch the day.

By winds that are sodden
    And have no heat,
Small garments are fluttered
    Above the street.

And this is the story
    The clotheslines tell:
A tenement house
    Where poor folks dwell.

MOON-RISE

Over the hill climbed the great red moon,
    Casting its ladder of night before;
And out from the straggling trees full soon,
    Shedding its glory the wide world o'er.

Round and ruddy and large and low,
    Tipping the trees with a glint of fire,
It then climbed onward, sure but slow,
    To the western gate of its heart's desire.

Smaller and brighter and farther away,
    More like the face of a silver shield;
And the beams came hurrying down to play
    'Mid the corn-rows standing along the field.

A SUBSTITUTE

The people of inventive mind,
    And those with penetration keen,
Are trying very hard to find
A substitute for gasoline.

But I have found it! So be calm!
    My substitute I'm using now.
The faithful tanner makes it from
The epidermis of a cow.

A BOTTLE OF INK

In speaking of poets and writers,
    The secret of writing, I think,
Depends a good deal upon knowing
    Just how to distribute the ink.

You purchase a bottle of Carter's,
    Removing the stopper or lid,
And there in that prison of blackness
    A hundred great poems are hid.

But here's what'll trouble you sorely,
    And fill all your being with doubt—
The problem of how you can manage
    To get all the great poems out.

First, get you a clean sheet of paper,
    Then dip your immaculate pen,
And keep on just like you were fishing—
    First writing, then dipping again.

136

The poem will nibble and nibble;
 You draw it out line after line;
And when it won't bite any longer,
 'Tis finished and ready to sign.

MORTARFICATION

In the year ninety-six—in the middle of May—
I was totin' up bricks an' a-earnin' my pay,
When along come a maid 'bout the size of a hoss,
An' there in the shade was a-chinnin' the boss.

She was leanin' with grace on a piece of a slat
By the side of the place where the mortar was at,
When the slat let loose with a terrible crack,
And she fell in the juice right flat on her back.

THE GOLDEN CALF

Old Aaron made a golden calf—
 He made it, I allow,
Because he hadn't gold enough
 To make a full-grown cow.

We're not much wiser than they were—
 Those Israelites of old.
We don't make ours up into calves,
 But still we worship gold.

OUR TROUBLES

Well, of course we're havin' trouble,
   An' of course we're feelin' bad;
But the future may jes' double
   What we done already had.

With a smile you better greet it—
   Start to whistle or to hum—
So you will have strength to meet it
   If the worst is yet to come.

VISITOR

I was busy when you came,
And the mention of your name
   Made me start;
And my slender train of thought,
Coming suddenly to naught,
   Fell apart.

With a momentary rise
Of resentment and surprise
   I was moved,
And I saw my ruined day
Slipping hurriedly away,
   Unimproved.

But the moment that you smiled
I was strangely reconciled
   To my plight;
And before you went away
I was asking you to stay
   Over-night.

IF PEOPLE ONLY WOULD BE KIND

If people only would be kind,
What happiness we all might find!
At home, abroad, where'er we go,
Just being kind would help us so.

If no one said an unkind word,
And no complaints were ever heard,
How much of misery we'd miss
By such a simple plan as this!

If we would smile instead of frown,
And keep our fiery tempers down,
Then other folks would do the same,
And none would criticize or blame.

If folks would more forgiving be
When little faults they chance to see,
Then they would be forgiven too
When something wrong they chanced to do.

If folks would love instead of hate,
The world's improvement would be great.
What happiness we all might find
If people only would be kind!

WINTER WIND

I am never easy when the north wind blows;
    I am never happy when the stars are cold.
Something like the shadow of unseen woes
    Haunts me in a manner that can't be told.

139

THE MODERN WAY

Brother, if you would be wise
    As a modern poet,
Clothe an old thought in such guise
    That no one will know it.
Everything has once been said,
    Many times been stolen,
And the stream of books is spread
    To a flood high-swollen.
        Notwithstanding this is true,
        People read—and call it new.

Rhyming brother, hear my song—
    If you wish to capture
Every one who comes along
    With your rhythmic rapture,
Be not over-apt to pen
    Everything so plainly.
Drop a hint just now and then,
    But leave it guess-work mainly.
        He is counted great who sings
        Unintelligible things.

PROFIT AND LOSS

Some folks are always so afraid
That they'll get cheated in a trade,
They'll use a dollar's worth of time
In figuring to save a dime.

While others, lest a bargain slip,
Will run and grab it the first clip,
To find, when they have got their wind,
That they've been very nicely skinned.

TO A HYPOCRITE

I will have to admit
You're a good hypocrite,
And you carry the signs of the trade:
You are sneaking and sly,
With a look in your eye
That honesty never has made.

When you pass for a saint
(Which you certainly ain't),
You have got to be careful, my son.
You're an actor, 'tis true,
And I'm bragging on you,
But your acting is over-done.

FOR SHERRY

This verse is for Sherry,
Who's always so merry—
Refusing to borrow
The uncertain sorrow
That may come tomorrow,
But just being gay
With the joy of today.

NOVEMBER RAIN

Soft as the purr of a kitten asleep
    Tinkle the drizzling drops of rain,
Tender as tears from skies that weep
    Over the ruin on hill and plain.

141

NOT BY BREAD ALONE

They wonder what I do for bread,
    Because I am so poor;
But I go by with lifted head,
As proud as one but lately fed,
    And faith that holds secure.
I do not live by bread alone—
    I fill myself with peace;
And every ill that I have known
Has changed to certain good and grown
    By magical increase.

They wonder what I do for wine
    In such an arid land;
But never once do I repine,
For all of heaven's brew is mine,
    And ready to my hand.
I do not thirst like other men—
    I drink the flaming sun,
And quaff the foaming stars, and then
I shall not ever thirst again
    Till age on age is done.

THE PERFECT MAN

The man who dresses very plain,
And thinks a little with his brain,
And reasons right and understands,
And works a little with his hands;

Who makes the Golden Rule his guide,
And never gives away to pride,
And sings a little every day,
And takes a little time to pray;

Who keeps a bridle on his tongue
And says no harm of old or young,
And helps no scandal on its way
By telling what he's heard 'em say.

Whose word is equal to his bond,
And goes a little way beyond,
And will no confidence betray,
Nor act the hypocrite for pay;

Who rates his honor as a man
As high as anybody can,
And loves his wife and pays his debts,
And smiles a heap and never frets—

If you have seen a man like that,
I wish you'd tell me where he's at,
And show me how to find the place,
And let me see his blessed face.

LEFT ALONE

I did not know how large a place
    You filled in my existence
Until your sweet and lovely face
    Had faded in the distance.

I could not shake your little hand
    Nor kiss you when we parted;
But surely you could understand
    That I was broken-hearted.

I could not trust my wayward lips
    With formal farewell speeches,
Lest I reveal, by awkward slips,
    How far the heart-string reaches.

143

You took the sunshine with you, dear,
 And joy went sailing after;
You left no hint of gladness here,
 Nor any sound of laughter.

AUTUMN LEAVES

The parent tree in sorrow grieves
In autumn for the falling leaves.
The leaves lie helpless on the ground,
All sodden wet and winter-bound.

Then comes the clean-up time in spring,
With rakes and hose and everything;
And I'm the one who frets and grieves
Because I have to rake the leaves.

HONEYSUCKLES

Forget, O Lord, the struggle and the pain,
 Forget the scars of battle that I bear;
So much of it was purposeless and vain—
 So much that failed to get me anywhere.

Forget, O Lord, the trouble and the tears,
 The bitter disappointments all along;
The squandered moments and the wasted years,
 And all the careful plans that ended wrong.

But on life's gladness let Thy record dwell,
 And put down all the moments of delight;
And, Lord, remember how I loved the smell
 Of honeysuckles in the summer night.

REST

Friend, if you have also met
Grief and sorrow and regret,
Fold your hands upon your breast
And enjoy a little rest.

Do not dwell upon the deed
Or the action that will lead
To the old regrets again—
Thoughts that torture you with pain.

Wave your hand and send them back
On the old forgotten track.
You are weary—it is best
That you sit down now and rest.

Close your eyes and calm your brain
And forget the driven rain,
While you dream of pleasant days—
Sunshine and the flowery ways.

Quaff the nectar of repose
From the red heart of the rose.
You are weary—it is best
That you sit down now and rest.

THE SIREN

Ambition, on forbidden ground,
   With finger bent and beckoning,
But if you disobey the Law
   There'll be a speedy reckoning,
And you must pay, in blood and tears,
   For every evil deed.

145

VANITY OF VANITIES

Vainglorious man
Will scheme and plan
Throughout his life's allotted span,
That he may claim
For his poor name
An hour's evanescent fame.

But look! Behold,
When all is told,
His name, though carven deep and bold,
By slow decay
Shall fade away,
And fame's allurements—where are they?

THE YEARS AHEAD

When all the years
Of blood and tears
Have dragged their torture through,
We'll have instead
The years ahead
To build the world anew.

We'll then prepare
To build it fair,
This world of yours and mine.
It isn't hate
That makes us great,
But only love divine.

146

SOUL-SCULPTURE

See the true sculptor by his marble block!
  The mallet and the chisel long he plies;
How strangely disappears the rugged rock!
  How strangely does the speaking image rise!

O foolish man that cleavest to the clay!
  Thy soul is on the selfsame basis built;
'Tis thine to hew the offending parts away;
  'Tis thine to shape into what form thou wilt.

SUNSET

I

All fair and cloudless was the day;
  The sun-bright skies no shadow knew;
Along the West at evening lay
  The pure interminable blue.
But he who watched upon the height
  To see the sunset's glory come,
Was strangely reft of his delight,
  And strangely, sorrowfully dumb.

II

All day, before the wet wind's wrath,
  The angry clouds were tossed and rolled,
Till sunset blazed a shining path,
  And all the West was sudden gold.
Then he who watched the weeping day
  Die out in splendor so divine,
Knew in a dim, unconscious way,
  How tears can make sad faces shine.

SOUL IN PRISON

He had the voice of all the nightingales,
    And glimpsed the glory of the prophet's dream,
But spent himself in ineffective wails
    Against the hell that had to be his theme.

He was a tuned harp ready for the hour
    When blessed Israel should wake and sing;
But took strange orders from an alien power
    That knew no song nor any sacred thing.

He knew the language of the Morning Stars—
    Could fly with Gabriel or the Cherubim;
But uttered curses through his prison bars
    At those whose ignorance imprisoned him.

LOOKING BACKWARD

From out the mould'ring casket of dead years,
    That, wrapped in dust, has long and lonesome lain
    Within some unlit closet of the brain,
There peeps a boyish face, all wet with tears.

He turns upon me with an eager gaze,
    And cries, "Oh, Sir, why knowest not thou me?"
    I look—and in that eager face I see
And recognize myself of former days.

THE BUILDING OF DELPHA

The first who came to Delpha
    Was good Ebenezer Grimes,
Who immigrated hither
    In the Puritanic times.
He walked into the ancient wood
    With courage and with pride,
Hewed down the trees and built a house
    To shelter his young bride.

And then he settled down to work—
    To plow and plant and reap;
His days were filled with honest toil,
    His nights with peaceful sleep.
He cleared the pines from off the hill
    That slopes up to the west;
Then he was old and full of years
    And he laid down to rest.

But there were Abner, Seth and Will
    To take their father's place,
To propagate the species
    And to multiply the race;
And so they built them each a house
    And married each a wife,
And settled down there side by side
    To meet the needs of life.

The fields were broadened year by year
    Fast as the children grew,
And soon the little settlement
    Had numbered thirty-two;
For while the old men bent with age,
    Up rose their gallant sons—
The young men took the old men's place,
    And thus the story runs.

The little church you see out there
    Was built in years long gone
When Abner's grandson Malachi
    Was full of life and brawn;
But he has gone to take his place
    In silence long and deep
In that old graveyard near the church
    Where all the Grimeses sleep.

But stranger folk from distant parts
    Had come to Delpha then—
A troop of slender little dames
    And anxious, bustling men—
And they had laid out splendid streets
    Across the goodly fields,
And there were hammers keeping time
    To hum of factory wheels.

And I, Rudolphus Rastus Grimes,
    The great-grandson of Will,
Am creeping up and down among
    These modern wonders still;
But soon there'll be another mound
    Beneath the churchyard tree,
And then proud Delpha will forget
    My ancestors and me.

THE LIVES OF MEN

The lives of men are little sailing ships
    That sail forever under unknown skies,
The question of all questions at their lips,
    The wonder of all wonders in their eyes.

The winds of time are blowing toward the west;
    The sails are set and every ship must go
Forever forward on its unknown quest—
    Into what storms and terrors none may know.

They cannot turn, as turn the merchant fleets,
    And come again with treasures from afar,
Nor meet out-going vessels as one meets
    Familiar faces at the harbor bar.

Howbein they are many that embark,
    They shall not be companions on the way;
But each alone shall stumble through the dark,
    And each alone shall hurry through the day.

The lives of men are tragic little flocks
    Of silent little ships that onward wend.
The lonesome lost winds drive them on the rocks,
    And death receives them at the journey's end.

AS THE SPIRIT MOVES

Today I have hammered out page after page
    Of poems that surely will sell.
Tomorrow I'll read them and wonder what sage
    Could have writ so remarkably well.

Today I've been silent—had nothing to say—
    And callers pronounced me a dunce.
Tomorrow I'll be very jolly and gay,
    And talk to a dozen at once.

MEN WORKING

Little sign standing
On the right-of-way;
Loud letters telling
What it has to say.

Men around the corner
Working on the grade,
Mending and repairing
For the traveller's aid.

Pull around the sign-board,
Bear to the right—
(They'll hang a red lantern
Up here tonight.)

Dirty men working
With a greasy machine—
(We'll have a good road,
And we'll keep clean.)

AN IDLE MOMENT

One hill, two hills, three hills,
  And a valley for every one;
And over beyond the last hill
  Sinks the sun.

One mile, two miles, three miles,
  And there is a winding road
Where a motor-truck is toiling
  With its load.

152

THE BURDEN-BEARER

In devious ways I've wandered
    And many dark paths trod,
And deeply have I pondered
    The hidden things of God.

Much of my life I've wasted
    On paltry things and vain,
And often have I tasted
    The bitter dregs of pain.

And still the same old grinding
    And tedious tasks return.
Is there no hope of finding
    The rest for which I yearn?

ASPIRATION

Beyond the pales of speech I wandered far,
Under the Evening Star,
And held sweet converse with the spirit band
That guards the Sunset Land.

For where the human tongue is speechless, there,
Hard by the Mount of Prayer,
The Universal Soul, unfettered, springs
Straight to the heart of things.

Transcending every tie that men have known,
Mounting aloft, alone,
To the far heaven-land of spirit-thought
Where carnal things are naught.

And there, transfigured past all human kin,
Shaming the dreams of men,
The soul its true affinity may find
In the Eternal Mind.

For, lo the shapes that bind us to the earth
Are of so little worth,
Compelling us as prisoners to grope
Unto the gates of hope.

What need to fret behind the prison bars
When there are suns and stars,
And Wisdom, standing in her palace gate,
Beckons us while we wait?

There is a depth of consciousness profound
That only God can sound;
There is a height o'ertopping human speech
That only God can reach.

And in this fuller presence of the truth
I find perpetual youth,
And there my dreams are ripened and my soul
Mounts to its truer goal.

HEROIC LIVING

To some it may be gratifying
To think about heroic dying;
But those who in such manner view it
Are willing other men should do it.

I like the man who's daily giving
His thought to high heroic living,
To make world-peace so never-ending
That none need die in its defending.

154

MY MIRROR

I still have the mirror I got
    Long years ago;
But something's the matter, and what—
    I don't know.

It showed me at first as a youth,
    And in my prime,
And I'm certain it told the truth
    For a time.

But—what do you think?—today
    When I looked in,
It showed me as wrinkled and gray
    As old sin.

Such terrible lying to me
    Is very bold.
I reckon that mirror must be
    Getting old.

THE BEAN-POD

A bean-pod, lost from its brothers,
    Went to sleep on the ground,
And the damp earth loved the bean-pod
    And folded its wet arms 'round.

And there was a strange conception—
    The strangest that ever was seen;
A little sunbeam was the midwife,
    And lo, the birth of a bean.

RADIO

A man across on t'other hill
    Yelled "Hello thar!" to me,
And I could hear each word he said
    As plain as plain could be.

"I'm goin' to stretch a fencin' wire
    On poles," says he, and smiles,
"Then you an' me can talk on that
    For mosta dozen miles."

Of course I knowed it wouldn't work—
    At least, the chance was small;
But when he got his wire strung up,
    It did work, after all.

"Hold on," sez I, "don't let success
    Completely crack your lid.
You'll never talk a hundred miles;
    It simply can't be did."

But, bless yer soul, that crazy man,
    With bales of wire unfurled,
Kept on at work till he at last
    Talked half around the world.

"All right," sez I, "you're pretty smart,
    That much I will admit.
But I am sure the limit's reached,
    And so I guess you'll quit."

Deliberately he cut the wires
    And let the poles stand bare,
Then talked around the earth an' back
    Jist on the naked air.

A SONG OF HOPE

This is what I always say
    When the storm-clouds rise:
There will come another day,
    Bringing brighter skies.

This is how I always feel
    When the troubles start:
Time's a doctor that can heal
    Every wounded heart.

Mighty hard to bear the pain
    For a little while;
But when peace has come again
    We'll learn how to smile.

What is that I hear you cry?—
    Grief has laid you low?
You'll feel better by and by—
    It is always so.

THE OLD FOLKS ARE A-KEEPING HOUSE YET

Oh, it's been a-many a day
Since the children went away,
Leaving memories that we never can forget.
Some have moved off to the West;
Some have died and gone to rest,
But the Old Folks are a-keeping house yet.

It's the same old chairs they keep
That have rocked us all to sleep,
And they sit around the same hearthstone;
And they put the milk to turn
In the same old wooden churn,
And they must be mighty lonesome all alone.

Up the old familiar lane
They're a-walking with a cane,
And I know their aged eyes are often wet;
And I guess they wish and yearn
For their children to return,
But the Old Folks are a-keeping house yet.

THINGS THAT COME NO MORE

Alas, that as the seasons sped,
I have been too concerned for bread,
And have not taken time to see
The many flowers that bloomed for me.

The apple tree will always bloom,
The rose send out its rare perfume.
There'll be no end of springs ahead,
But some new spring will find me dead.

I've missed the sight of many things
That come back with returning springs;
But more than these I now deplore
The loss of things that come no more.

Come with me, dear, and let us look
For alder tags along the brook;
And somewhere, peeping from the ground,
The sweet arbutus will be found.

There will be larks when we are gone
To serenade the gates of dawn,
And other men and other maids
Will wander through the evening shades.

WHEN SLEEPERS WAKE

The sleeping brain is oft inspired
With visions much to be desired
   To hold and keep.
'Twere worth a crown if one could write
The shadow-poems of the night
   When sleepers sleep

There would be angels fair of face,
Arrayed in robes of liquid lace,
   And crowned with peace,
Disporting nightly on the shore
Of some eternal Nevermore
   Where troubles cease.

There would be dreams of tables spread
With fabled wealth of holy bread
   And pleasant wine,
And dreaming rivers flowing down
From holy mount to holy town
   In lands divine.

But dreams of night will never stay
To face the open light of day
   For poet's sake.
In playful mood they fade and change
To shapes impossible and strange
   When sleepers wake.

A FRIEND

A friend who is worthy the name that he bears
   Is one who will stay by your side
When great tribulations come down unawares
   And you are sore tempted and tried.

MOVE OVER

At working time, when young and strong,
  I took my place with brawny men.
The work was hard, the day was long,
  But I was built to stand it then.
And oft I did, with due regard,
    Some wearier worker's task assume,
      Calling out
      With a shout:
"Move over, old pard, if your labor is hard;
  Move over and give me room."

At eating time, with hunger keen,
  And appetite that never failed,
A better "hand" was seldom seen
  Where cooks and cookery prevailed.
I'm far too modest now to state
    Just how much food I did consume.
      But my tongue
      Fairly sung:
"Move over, old mate, and pass me a plate—
  Move over and give me room."

At sleeping time, with muscles tired,
  And all relaxed from labor's grind,
With all my heart I then desired
  The softest bunk that I could find;
But sought some handy place to drop
    And snooze away the midnight gloom;
      And expressed
      My request:
"Move over, old top, and share me your flop;
  Move over, and give me room."

At dying time, when life is spent,
   With mind and body all played out,
I'll make my bow and go content,
   With not a question or a doubt.
As breath departs and speech suspends,
   I'll say to those within the tomb,
   Speaking low,
   As I go:
"Move over, old friends, for my pilgrimage ends;
   Move over, and give me room."

LIFE MUST GO ON

Great Mystery of Life! The sentiment spring
Whence flows the hope of every living thing;
Through which unliving matter finds its soul
And drives ahead to some eternal goal.
In the beginning, Life! And from that day
The living stream has broadened on its way,
Nor halted once, nor for a moment lost
The great initiative. At all cost,
   Life must go on.

A thousand conquerors may come and go,
Filling the earth with agony and woe,
And breeding pestilence and nameless fear,
Till one might think the utter end was near.
But in that seeming rout, that darkest hour,
Life has reserves of unsuspected power.
Though death stride heavily across the earth,
There yet will be the miracle of birth—
   Life must go on.

Though fire and flood and earthquake do their worst,
And men go mad with hunger and with thirst;
Though love be lost and wealth and honor pass,
And words of comfort are but sounding brass;
Though all Four Horsemen ride at breathless pace
And death appears to win the sorry race;
Though blood run rivers till the seas are red,
And earth be pocked with tombing of the dead—
    Life must go on.

What is this Life that will not call it quits,
Though hearts be broke and souls be torn to bits?
What is this Life that will not fail and die?
The wise ones know no more than you and I.
And all we know is that the time of need
Calls to its aid the strong eternal Seed.
Defying all the powers that hurt and kill,
It has survived till now, and always will.
    Life must go on.

SCULPTOR'S TOOLS

You are a builder of flesh and bone,
    Using the tools of the master Mind.
No man thinks to himself alone;
    He thinks aloud to all mankind.

Thoughts are hammers and chisels too,
    Shaping the face for good or ill.
Some tear down what others do;
    Some build up with a careful skill.

Vile thoughts wrinkle and twist the face,
    Making it hard and coarse and old.
Pure thoughts give it a shining grace—
    Youth's glad laughter and beauty's mold.

THE CONGRESSIONAL LIBRARY

A dream in polished marble! This thou art,
  O temple of the living and the dead!
The beauty charms the eye and wins the heart,
  As through thy halls thy thousand lights are shed.

Oft have I stood upon thy central stair
  And felt the thrill that hath no outward voice;
A million heavenly beauties mingling there
  Compel the eager student to rejoice.

Man's most sublime conception, highest thought,
  Converges there with something of the skill
By which the circling suns were formed and taught
  To roll submissive to their Maker's will.

I've wandered through thy spacious halls by day,
  And viewed, with well-pleased eye, thy mural charms—
Thy living mottoes, writ in classic way,
  Thy pictured muses with uncovered arms.

Again I've sought thee as the twilight fell,
  When thou wert bathed in soft electric light,
And 'mid thy million books (I love them well),
  I've whiled away the early hours of night.

O living world of dead men's better selves—
  Thou world of books—my heart would dwell with thee!
Fain would I walk amid thy endless shelves
  And hear thy voices calling unto me.

Here dwells the best that every age has known,
  The gathered treasures of recorded time;
Here, framed in the abiding strength of stone,
  Our legacy, eternal and sublime.

THE ORGAN OF LIFE

Over and over and over
    Monotonous voices call
Till weariness creeps upon us
    And slumb'rous eyelids fall;
And dreamily then we finger
    The dissonant, rasping keys,
And little we think of the terror
    That trembles along the breeze.

On the organ of life we are playing—
    Each life is a separate tune,
And one is a dirge of the winter,
    And one is a carol of June;
But all of our chords are minor—
    There are notes that we cannot reach
Till we finish the lesson that only
    The Master of life can teach.

There might have been more of music
    If we had but taken heed
To the hungering eyes that question
    And the sorrowful hearts that bleed;
And there might have been more of sweetness
    To mellow the harsh discord
If we had thought more of the service
    And less of the servant's reward.

THIS HUMAN RACE

What puny thing is this that dares to throw
    A challenge full into his Maker's face,
And turn creator of a world and go
    Careering forth into the fields of space?

164

Seeing that out of nothing he can make
    Substantial things to answer his behest,
What wild adventures might he undertake?
    What hidden worlds be conquered and possessed?

No suppliant pleading for a little gift,
    He claims the universe by right divine,
And probes the dark where unknown systems drift,
    And finds his way where new-born planets shine.

He grasps the hair of time and holds it back
    Till East and West surrender and agree,
And lays a line upon the thunder's track,
    And measures the unmeasurable sea.

But he whose far-flung genius might arouse
    The jealousy of God on heaven's throne,
Is yet a doddering fool in his own house,
    And cannot feed himself nor rule his own.

MY THOUGHT OF YOU

I have the sweetest thought of you,
    But don't know how to word it;
For no tongue ever shaped it true,
    And no ear ever heard it.

The loves of all forgotten years
    Are gathered in the story
With all the memories and tears,
    And all the shouts of glory.

But it is deeper than they all,
    And infinitely sweeter,
As if the sparrow's mating call
    Were drowned in liquid meter.

165

Ah, language has its proper sphere,
But lovers do not need it.
My thought of you is written here—
Look in my eyes and read it.

ARE YOU THROUGH FOR THE DAY?

Are you through for the day? Have you finished?
    Is there nothing else waiting to do?
And is somebody's trouble diminished?
    And is somebody thankful to you?

Can you go to sleep now? Can you slumber
    With a conscience that judges you right?
Is there no guilty thought to encumber
    You agreeable dreams of the night?

Are you through for the day? Are you certain
    You have done all the good that you can?
As the night covers you with its curtain,
    Do you feel like an innocent man?

JUST LOOK

I don't want to tell you a thing;
    I just want to show you the view
That greets me these mornings in spring
    When nature is garmented new.

I don't want to limit your sight
    With any device of a book.
Don't wait for my fingers to write—
    Just stand at my elbow and look.

166

Sonnets

ONE HEAVENLY HOUR

The sun's last shining arrow from the west
Broke silently against old ivied walls;
The brown wren dreaming in her hidden nest,
The far, faint sound of moon-lit waterfalls.
A hammock swung between old mossy trees
My tired form resting in its friendly folds;
A book to read or handle as I please,
And all the charm that summer twilight holds.

O vanished years! I yet remember well
One heavenly hour of such a sacred night,
And how the perfumed shadows, as they fell,
Touched every fancied wrong and made it right;
While I lay listening, 'neath a friendly star,
To love-sick notes of Blanche's soft guitar.

OCTOBER DAYS

These are the days that come on silent feet,
Like mourners in a house where lie the dead,
When autumn's gathered glory is complete
And all the fevered world of brown and red
Is waiting for its beauty to be shed
In lavish waste upon the frosted ground—
A captive princess unto prison led,
A bride unhusbanded, a queen uncrowned.

These are the days of silence and sad smiles,
The mellow, memoried evening of the year,
When garnered harvest in abundant piles
Can scarce restrain the slow, unbidden tear.
Half-dreaming world, too rare for poet's praise—
So sweet, so sad, the dear October days.

UNTAMED

What shall I do with all my wayward dreams?
They are so many and so hard to hold.
They drift around me like dim shadow-streams
And whisper secrets that were never told.
And I, with all a poet's careful skill,
Attempt to catch them in a net of words;
But just beyond my reach they flutter still,
Or vanish like the shadow of swift birds.

They are the naked spirits of dumb songs
Set searching through creation for a voice;
But they are wild with memories of great wrongs
That kept them from the poet of their choice.
Forever thus they fret me night and day—
Unbodied thoughts that laugh and run away.

CATHEDRAL PINES

The holy pines that worship on the hill
Have built a dim cathedral of their own,
More beautiful than any carven stone,
More touched with magic of creative skill
And classic lines to match the Maker's will.
A feathered choir sends up to heaven's throne
Music more rare than any organ tone,
Bidding the world to listen and be still.

One tallest pine of all the sacred grove
Goes towering up, a great cathedral spire;
An humbler tier the arching splendor bears.
Glinting through lights and shadows interwove,
The new-grown twigs, with passionate desire,
Stand yearning up like little tender prayers.

TO THE FIGURES ON A GRECIAN URN

Think not, fair figures on the Grecian Urn,
'Tis immortality that you have won,
Nor hold it true that while the ages run
Your empty town must wait for your return.
O marble maid, not always will you spurn
Your lover's kiss till wooing time be done.
O marble lover, e'en the dying sun
Will, like your old spent passions, cease to burn.

For time enough will eat your urn to dust,
Denude your carven trees of every leaf,
And send you at the wind's will flying free.
Be patient, then, as marble creatures must,
And nurse no more your old unhappy grief—
The day comes surely when you shall not be.

PERPETUAL SACRIFICE

Go count the millions of forgotten dead
On all the battlefields that followed Cain,
And mark how certainly their blood was shed
For causes that were meaningless and vain;
How victory turns to ultimate defeat,
And evil purposes are evil still,
And how the Marnes and Verduns must repeat
On many a red and roaring Bunker Hill.

Age after age, in Liberty's fair name,
The old perpetual sacrifice is made;
And while the thrones disintegrate in flame,
The hopes of men forever fail and fade.
O sons and lovers, butchered like the swine,
How fares the land that drank your crimson wine?

171

ONE-TALENT MAN

God gave one little talent to his keeping—
A barren thing—the doubtful gift of song.
Day after day, heart-sick and spent with weeping,
He cried his wares to all the heedless throng.
They tossed him fame as oft a careless penny
Is flung to any beggar in the street.
(The beggars are so hungry and so many,
And who should worry if they do not eat?).

They found him starving on a mouldy crust—
(So small a harvest for so great a reaping.)
They gave him back to silence and to dust,
And on the slab whereunder he lies sleeping
They carved a line to hold his fame in trust:
"God gave one little talent to his keeping."

EROSION

When I have rested dead a thousand years,
Till frost and rain have weathered down the hill—
Till my dead dust as surface sand appears,
And down eroded ruts my ashes spill—
The brook will take me to its singing heart
And bear me on triumphant to the sea,
Till every land shall claim a little part,
And naught can be identified as me.

Will I be gone? Or will my dust return
From all the washing of the seven seas,
To find my lost identity and learn
To make new verses as I now make these?
If Gabriel wakes a poet when he blows,
I'll all be back together, I suppose.

MORE THAN POWER

Long did the kings and potentates conspire
To take by force the dwelling-place of man;
To build on Blood and dedicate with Fire,
And justify by Fear their awful plan.
Love was a little waif that Mercy found
Bleeding and lost upon a battered hill.
Her cause ignored, her gentle voice was drowned
In all the din of conflict raging still.

But when their Power had wrought its own defeat,
And when their Fire had burned their kingdoms down,
They came to Love, in penitence complete,
And placed upon her head creation's crown.
And so did Love, which seemed so weak and small,
Become at last the greatest Power of all.

BEAUTY AND PAIN

Whene'er I look on any lovely thing—
A landscape or a garden or a face—
Or when sweet music's dreamy murmuring
Is wafted to me in some quiet place,
Somewhere inside there comes a happy pain—
A glad, ecstatic feeling of regret—
That rises up and tingles through each vein,
As if despair and blessedness had met.

I know not why the goblet of delight
Is always flavored the taste of tears,
Nor why the face of beauty is not quite
The unalloyed good that it appears.
But this I know—that Beauty is most wise
When she appeals and hurts—and satisfies.

WILD GARDEN

So prim and proper in its guarded close,
With all its hedges trimmed exactly right;
With perfect plants all set in perfect rows
And not a weed nor rebel thing in sight:
It well may be the gardener's delight
To tend and keep it subject to his will,
Demanding, as it does, an endless fight
With wild and evil things that he must kill.

But never did a garden love its keeper
Nor give itself quite freely to his hand.
Its heart is wild; its jungle sense is deeper
Than its fine manners all so bravely planned.
Turn any garden loose—it will depart
And seek its level in the jungle's heart.

THEOCRITUS

Come, O Theocritus, and sing once more
As long in Syracuse thy voice was heard.
Bring back the melody of brook and bird,
The calling sea, the answer from the shore,
The fragrance of lost meadows, and restore
Thy shepherd lads and their forgotten sheep,
Thy singing reapers going forth to reap,
And all the rose-crowned loves that we adore.

For we are fallen now on evil days—
Thin famine days that starve the Sacred Nine—
That know not Pan nor Daphnis, but upraise
Their guilty hands at Mammon's golden shrine.
Time-weary earth, in all her traveled ways,
Is thrilled no more with such a song as thine.

HOLY GRAIL

Reach forth your hand, my love. Take hold and drain
This brimming cup of nature's perfect brew;
Then at the fountain fill the cup again
And let me drink—but only after you.
So is the water changed to holy wine
Inside the cup your precious lips have pressed.
The common world is suddenly divine,
And I sit feasting here as heaven's guest.

No Launfal's dream, no Galahad's wild race,
No foot-sore wanderings in unknown lands—
But this clear fountain, your reflected face,
And this full cup to touch your lips, your hands.
And such the alchemy your fingers hold
That common iron shall blossom into gold.

WORDS

You know the power of words—how masters find
A million combinations for their speech,
And how the tones and colors, so combined,
Create a rainbow path of endless reach
On which their thoughts may travel to the last
High-vaulted heaven of the mind's delight,
Leaving our lesser minds below, out-classed,
And beaten in the overwhelming fight.

Yet should I have all genius at its peak,
And tax all languages for praises new,
I should not find, though I forever seek,
The perfect word to tell the charm of you.
My heart, my soul, my very being's core,
Should still in wordless wonderment adore.

BURDEN OF PITY

Only one thing has made me wish to die—
Not any pain nor danger of my own;
No earthly dread, no portent from the sky,
Flaming its message of a doom unknown.
Fearless I stand, calm as a forest oak,
Daring the worst that fate can do to me;
Eager for life—to sniff its battle-smoke,
To tread its earth or sail its bitter sea.

But seeing how all nature writhes in pain—
Human and brute, and graduated down—
And how my little strength were spent in vain
To lift one thorn of all its thorny crown:
Oppressed with pity's overwhelming tide,
How oft it had been comfort to have died!

RELATIVITY

Some things to us are infinitely great,
While other things are infinitely small,
And, past infinitude, still others wait
Whose size we cannot comprehend at all.
The rainbow arch that crowns the misty hill
When bridegroom sun has kissed his weeping bride,
Is formed of shining drops that carry still
The structure of a universe inside.

The watery atom has its proton sun
'Round which electron planets wheel and spin;
It has its million ages that are done
Before our earthly minute can begin.
Our earth is but a mist-drop in a bow
That spans a heaven greater than we know.

NEW CREATION

I have destroyed the evil world—blotted it out—
Swept clean the endless reaches of great space,
Till all the searching winds might run and shout
Vainly to find somewhere its hidden place.
I have suddenly unmade the nightmare lands,
Heavy with armies, bitter and loud with hate;
Rebuked old coward Satan till he stands
Disarmed and trembling for his hapless fate.

Then with a sudden splendor of new light
I've dreamed a great new heaven on the earth;
Made angels ready for their maiden flight,
And built high thrones for righteousness and worth.
And now, beloved—faithful ones and true—
Enter and live! I made it all for you.

AN APRIL NIGHT AT FORD'S THEATER

To laugh away the crowding cares of state,
And charge again in one forgetful hour
The war-spent battery of psychic power
That fed his dreaming soul and made him great:
For this came Lincoln to his hour of fate,
With unseen danger lurking to devour,
While beauty's pageantry and fashion's flower
Around his solemn figure throng'd elate.

His sad, prophetic eyes, so used to tears,
Where Melancholy's ghost was wont to dwell—
A moment's Comedy had come to seek.
A flash! A scream! And the unfolding years
Had claimed him their immortal as he fell,
Transfixed on Tragedy's eternal peak.

IF LOVE WERE JUST A WORD

If Love were just a word made out of air,
And cold and calculating and afraid,
With no hot tempest of great joy to share
With one beloved and for such sharing made:
Then would the word be meaningless to men—
Some abstract idea captured in a sound;
Some worthless exercise of tongue and pen,
Whose doubtful use no linguist had found.

But Love is not some word that people say;
It is the breath of life, the soul's strong wine,
And whoso drinks it for one deathless day
Shall be henceforth exalted and divine;
And he, despite his woundings and his scars,
Shall walk erect, his head among the stars.

REBELLION

So lightly holding motherhood's divinity
As something less than any idle tale,
She traded love to purchase black virginity,
And sold posterity to buy a veil.
Scorning a lover's passionate embraces
As all too carnal for a saint to bear,
She willed her body into prison places
And gave her soul to penance and to prayer.

But love surrenders to no stated plan;
The heart is not the servant of the will.
Her pagan flesh grew restless and began
To nurse the love that she had tried to kill—
Having forbidden thoughts about a man,
And dreaming of a cottage on a hill.

IN TIME OF HUNGER

I can go hungry and hold up my head—
Appear to men as if I fasted not;
Can bluff it through with nothing in the pot
And make believe that I am fully fed.
For I have other meat and other bread
That will sustain me in my secret plot
Against the gnawing hunger and the hot
Uneven battle with the day of dread.

But when my wife is hungry, when my child
Goes supperless and cries herself to sleep,
Then am I helpless; then is born the wild
Impulse to wring my hands and weep—
Confused, defeated, slow to understand
Why too much food breeds hunger in the land.

ONE CERTAIN DATE

Once in the long, long ages of the world,
Between the far beginning and the end,
Here on this potter's wheel together whirled,
A little hour of loving we may spend.
A thousand chances we had come alone,
With centuries of darkness in between;
Then had we not this vital moment known,
Nor face to face had I thy beauty seen.

But now that time has synchronized us so,
And flashed us on the screen of life together,
Let us enjoy the moments as they go,
Nor vainly tug at fate's unyielding tether.
If by misfortune we had missed the bus,
Who would have met this date—instead of us?

The Dream Lives On

THE LUCK OF A LOUSY CALF

My Uncle Jake's young daughter Kate
Got married to some sorry skate,
And went off with him in a Ford
To find a place where they could board.
They took their meals at some cafe,
And found a barn-loft full of hay
Where they could sleep beneath the beams,
With naught to break their happy dreams.

Now Uncle Jake and all the rest
Were deeply wounded and distressed,
And swore with many an ugly durn
That Kate should nevermore return.
They'd cut her off without a cent
Because she took that sorry gent,
And nary dime of that estate
Should ever pass on down to Kate.

So Kate and mate dropped out of sight,
And no one took the pains to write
And ask if they were still alive,
Or send a wish that they would thrive.
The cheap cafe was soon unknown;
The barn stood empty and alone;
And somewhere down the human stream
They drifted onward like a dream.

But somehow, as the seasons rolled,
The papers came back East and told
How in the West a certain guy
Was getting rich and living high.
For Kate and mate had staked a claim
Out where the oil gushers flame,
And their big gusher did not fail
Till they were lousy with the kale.

As soon as Uncle Jake was wise
To Kate's and mate's financial rise,
He melted like a tallow man
Dropped in a red-hot frying-pan.
And all the folks about the place
Grew strangely good and full of grace,
And said, with hands across the heart,
They always knew that Kate was smart.

The moral is that when you're broke
And hungry and about to croak,
The folks in country and in town
Will do their best to keep you down.
But if you buck the whole combine
And win out bit and brave and fine,
The doggon hypocrites will try
To eat you up like pumpkin pie.

KINDRED

I

I own my kinship with the weak,
    My brotherhood to hungry men
Who starve in garret dens and seek
    The poor hard earnings of the pen.

Divine debauchees, drunk with dreams,
    And holding hearts that burn and bleed;
Yet foiled in all their dearest schemes,
    And hounded down by every need.

Unworldly souls that seek the stars,
    And all mis-mated to the earth,
On whom life's lacerating scars
    Were branded from their day of birth.

184

Untimely prophets, half insane,
    But speaking still the prophet's word;
Whose ears are open to a strain
    That solemn sane men never heard.

I sing of these—the lonely breed
    That neither heaven nor earth will claim;
Who follow love's insistent lead
    And scorch their wings in beauty's flame.

II

My feet have rugged ways to go,
    But I don't notice how they ache
If one hand reaches out to Poe
    And one hand tethers me to Blake.

If Hayne and Timrod come along,
    And dear Lanier is in the crowd,
My own heart bubbles up with song
    And I am passionately proud.

If Dowson wants to be my chum;
    If Thompson needs me for a friend,
I'll go down with them to their slum
    And chance it with them to the end.

These great unhappy singing souls
    Have worked on me their magic charm.
They struggle toward their shining goals,
    And I go with them, arm in arm.

KNOWLEDGE

We know the distance to the sun,
   And what Uranus weighs;
Can figure how the planets run
   And where the comet stays.
But we can't trace an unkind word
   Through all its evil course,
Nor make amends to those who heard,
   Nor check its deadly force.

We know how far a ray of light
   Can travel in a year;
Can analyze it in its flight
   And make its meaning clear.
But we can't follow up a smile
   And see how far it shines,
Nor estimate it by the mile
   In radiating lines.

The moon is but an open book
   For everyone to know,
And on her pitted face we look
   And read her tale of woe.
But there are faces seamed with care
   That pass us every day;
We don't know what their owners bear,
   Nor what they'd like to say.

We visit with our neighbor Mars,
   As all good neighbors should;
Throw kisses at the Seven Stars
   And tell them to be good.
But we don't visit with the folks
   Who live across the street,
Nor help them bear their heavy yokes,
   Nor ask them in to eat.

Beyond our telescopic eyes,
  By gravity's decree,
We get position, weight and size
  Of worlds we cannot see.
But, oh, we do not try to find
  The secret hidden pain
That rankles in some quiet mind
  That never does complain.

We know the age-long wonder tale
  Of Saturn and his rings,
And follow Neptune's awful trail
  As on through space he swings.
But we don't know the bitter grief
  Our next-door neighbors bear;
And just to make it very brief,
  'Tis little that we care.

PORT-SEEKERS

Lone pilgrim bands,
  In Eastern lands,
Traverse Sahara's burning sands;
  O'er deserts wide,
  With weary stride,
They go to where the gods abide.

Foot-sore, the while,
  In endless file,
They cover many a pathless mile.
  Their gods, bedight
  In spectral white,
Drift ever from their aching sight.

Lo, far and wide,
On luring tide,
A myriad freighted vessels ride;
Within each hold
Is stored the gold
Of merchant-princes manifold.

They sail and sail
Through calm and gale,
But ne'er the long-sought harbor hail.
Their port of mist
Has flown, I wist,
Into the farther amethyst.

POSSESSION

World of old dead ages—
Battles long forgot—
I go walking by you
As if you were not.
Keep your bones and bludgeons—
All you ever knew;
Take your red hands off me—
I am not for you.

World of cave and jungle,
World of fang and claw,
Where the brute was master
And the club was law—
You may have attractions
Other men can see;
But I pass you over—
You are not for me.

World of smiling faces
World of tender eyes,
Where the strong are gentle
And the weak are wise;
Where the mind is master
And the heart is true;
World of truth and beauty—
I belong to you.

World of homes and gardens
Set by happy streams;
World of books and music,
Poetry and dreams,
Where the happy bird-songs
Gladden every tree,
World of love and laughter—
You belong to me.

OCTOBER'S SHOW

'Twould be a splendid story,
    If one might tell it true,
About the flaming glory
    October brings to view.

If one might be a master
    And capture nature's show
Before the great disaster
    Has dealt its fatal blow.

For hills so garbed in wonder,
    So bathed in beauty's smile,
Will be the spoiler's plunder
    In such a little while.

LIFE AND PEACE

This is life—to gaily plod
Where deep the plowshare turns the sod,
   And scatter seed,
And garner safe with thankful hand
The well-earned product of the land
   For future need.

This is peace—the toil that brings
Content, with all the simple things
   That life requires—
Sufficient food, a home, a friend,
And, crowning all, the abundant end
   Of small desires.

HERE IS WISDOM

Old Andy never went to school
   And never read a book;
But he who takes him for a fool
   Will need a second look.
He knows more things than any one
   That you'll be apt to meet,
And on all questions 'neath the sun
   His knowledge is complete.

Old Bobby went to school a bit,
   And he has read a heap,
And often keeps his candles lit
   While Andy lies asleep.
But Bobby isn't quite so sure
   Of quite so many things;
For questions rise and doubts allure,
   And faith has broken wings.

Old Jasper sports an LL.D.,
    And Ph.D. as well,
And every other high degree
    That colleges will sell.
But Jasper only shakes his head
    At questions great or small,
And seems to know, when truth is said,
    Not anything at all.

TODAY

Let the hills alone today;
They will stay.
They'll be ready for your rhyme
Any time.

And the mountains and the sea—
Let them be.
You can fill up future days
With their praise.

And the planets and the sun—
Let them run.
Though they light a distant tract,
They'll be back.

Better in the present hour
Smell a flower;
Better celebrate the rose
While it blows.

Better rhapsodize the brief
Autumn leaf,
Or the momentary bliss
Of a kiss.

Music dying on the air
Like a prayer,
Or a dreaming bird at rest
In its nest.

These, O Poet, strive to get
In your net;
For at some tomorrow's dawn
They'll be gone.

BEFORE AND AFTER YOU

This is my old ancestral place;
   I knew these hills before you came;
But I had never seen your face
   Nor heard your name.

The charm that later came with you
   Could not be missed before its birth;
I could not think of skies more blue,
   Or greener earth.

But now you seem so much a part
   Of all the things that I have known,
I have forgotten when my heart
   Lived here alone.

It seems that all enduring things
   Were built around you from of old—
As if the gold of Ophir springs
   From your heart's gold.

If you should leave this world today
   To fare along some other shore,
I think the world would pass away
   And be no more.

It seems impossible to think
    That birds and blossoms could remain
When death had broken such a link
    In nature's chain.

I cannot sense the singing brook,
    Nor how there yet can come a dawn,
Nor how the lonesome hills will look
    When you are gone.

CRAZY BEN

There was poor old Crazy Ben,
    Who has died and gone to rest.
He was not like other men,
    But he did his very best.

I have often heard it said
    (And I knew it from the start)
That the crazy in his head
    Didn't reach into his heart.

For I saw him every day,
    And I knew just where he stood.
In his simple-minded way
    He was always doing good.

Children trusted him at sight,
    And the dumb brutes were his friends.
If a heart was ever right,
    Surely it was Crazy Ben's.

But he lived his simple life
    In a very quiet way;
Never mixed in any strife—
    Never having much to say.

He was serving all his days,
    And but seldom he was served,
And he never got the praise
    That so richly he deserved.

It was spring when he was born,
    And the summer was his pride;
But his autumn was forlorn,
    And 'twas winter when he died.

And there were no bands to play,
    And there were no flags to wave;
But a chilling wind that day,
    When they bore him to his grave.

SUCH LITTLE THINGS

A little rain-drop in the sky
Was seen to blink its little eye,
As if it certainly would cry:
"I'm such a little drop of rain
That if I fell upon the plain,
I never would be seen again.
I'll just remain up in the sky
And let the other drops go by
To wet the earth that's very dry."

A little sunbeam crawled away
And hid himself one winter day,
And this is what they heard him say:
"I'm such a little puny light,
I'd not be noticed in the night,
And darkness gives me such a fright.
I think I will my duty shirk
And in this cozy corner lurk,
And let the others do the work."

And so the earth was starved and dry,
While every rain-drop in the sky
Moaned, "What a little drop am I!"
And so the world was in the dark
While every beam made this remark:
"Oh, I am such a tiny spark!"

WHEN RILEY DIED

This poem was begun at the time of Riley's death in 1916, but
it was put aside and not finished until later.

O Jim, are you gone? Have you crossed the divide?
Have you left us alone on the sorrowing side?
Can it possibly be that old Lockerbie Street
Will echo no more to the tramp of your feet?

The little white girl in the little white dress
Will walk through the street and enjoy it less;
And the dear little bird nesting under the eve
Will come out and listen and miss you and grieve.

The bullfrog that lives in the Old Swimmin' Hole
Will bellow more sadly, in sorrow of soul;
The poor lonesome crow will just sit on his limb,
And somehow the world will be different to him.

The sigh from the bosom of 'Lizabuth Ann
Will answer the moans of the Raggedy Man,
And poor Orphan Annie, although she is brave,
Will never be happy this side of the grave.

The lily that blooms by the cabin door
Will weep forever and smile no more;
As she fills her cup with the morning dew,
She will have no thought but the thought of you.

In the old hay-loft that you loved so well,
The ghost of a happier time will dwell,
And the hen's nests hidden beneath the hay
Will never be found till the judgment day.

There won't be much in the way of joy
For the old hound dog and the barefoot boy;
And the ripening wheat-fields, day nor night,
Will be no pleasure to Old Bob White.

The sleeping baby will roll and toss
And dream his personal sense of loss,
And every place where children play,
They'll know that Riley has passed away.

HOMER IN A GARDEN

A sheltered garden in a sheltered land,
    A pleasant seat upon the mossy ground;
A book of Homer open in my hand,
    And languorous sweet odors all around.

Then suddenly the ages fell away;
    My sheltered garden floated off in space,
And on some lost millennium's bloody day
    I stood with storied Ilium face to face.

The honeysuckle smells that would not fade
    Hung like a ghost above the field of red,
And every dreaming pansy-face was made
    The likeness of the faces of the dead.

Such wonders were abroad in all the land,
    Such magic did the mighty gods employ,
That every lily was a Helen's hand,
    And every rose a burning tower of Troy.

NEW BIRTH

Now when the pulse of time is low,
And life is but a broken thing,
Across the distance and the snow
There skims a wing.
An angel takes the dying year
And leaves the New Year in its stead,
And drops a tear
To bless the dead.

Now old mistakes are cancelled out,
And old regrets are put away,
And we will welcome with a shout
This better day—
This day in which hope sees a star,
And listening love can hear a song.
It isn't far!
It won't be long!

THE NIGHT

The Night is an ardent lover,
   His lady the Earth,
And steadily hath he woo'd her
   Since time had birth.

The Night is a sad musician;
   His harp is the wind;
And the sear leaves dance to the music
   Till their ranks are thin'd.

So the Night hangs up his lantern—
   His lantern, the moon—
And he sings for the Earth, his lady,
   A slumb'rous tune.

He hath the stars for his jewels,
    And the dew for his tears,
And hath wept on his lady's bosom
    For a million years.

The night finds the lady waiting
    At the trysting place,
And he sprinkles the moonbeams over
    Her sleeping face.

And there by his lady's bower
    Safe watch he keeps
Till the wind-harps cease their sighing,
    And the hoot-owl sleeps.

THE POET IN HIS DEN

One night the poet sat and wept
    O'er grevious ills that burden'd him,
While all the world oblivious slept
    Beneath the shadows deep and dim.

"Give me a song, O Muse," he cried,
    "A song to move the world to tears;
Which rendered, I can better bide
    The thankless service of the years."

He lifted up his wond'rous harp,
    Whose vibrant chords were keen to speak;
He sang of competition sharp,
    Of how the strong oppressed the weak.

But all the slumb'rous world was still,
    And no man heard the tragic song;
No bosom sent an answering thrill
    Back to the bard, who waited long.

Again the chords were touched, and now
    War's agony rose loud and high—
The voice of bellowing guns, and how
    Men marched away from home to die.

Up rose the world with morn's return,
    The song was lost in traffic's roar;
The critic's voice was harsh and stern,
    So that the bard could sing no more.

A little child with beaming face
    Found out the poet's lonely den;
Brought glad new life into the place,
    And he was moved to sing again.

This time it was a soft, sweet song
    Of childhood's tender, trusting years;
But when the bard looked up, ere long,
    Behold, the world was all in tears.

SMOTHERED FIRES

We meet today as we have met before,
    And pass some formal words and drift apart;
Then silence and the closing of a door,
    And just a nameless hunger in the heart.

The words we say are born upon the lips—
    The lips that close against the heart's desire;
Our seeking souls forever in eclipse,
    Our flame of passion but a smothered fire.

Strange words and stranger silences will fall
    Ghost-like across the ever-changing years,
And the dim memory of dead days will call,
    And there will be no answer but our tears.

THE PROPHET

The prophet lived in a little town,
And all the people cried him down.
They killed him because of his dangerous views—
For I read about it in the Daily News.

A few years later, when hate was spent,
Somebody built him a monument,
And there were those who called him clean—
For I read about it in a magazine.

A thousand years—and the people came
And bowed and prayed in the prophet's name;
His praises rang till the heavens shook—
For I read about it in a little book.

THE WRECKERS

Today, as I went walking soon,
Before the noon,
I passed an old house in the town,
Near fallen down.

And men were working on the wall,
So soon to fall;
For they were just a wrecking crew
With work to do.

I watched them as each heavy stroke
Some timbers broke;
I listened as, with crashing knell,
The rafters fell.

I touched the foreman on his sleeve:
"Sir, by your leave,
Are these good wreckers highly skilled
If one should build?"

"Oh, no indeed," the foreman said,
And shook his head.
"These wreckers know one only art—
To tear apart.

"Where other men have labored long
And builded strong,
These wreckers in a day or so
Can lay it low."

MAD ADVENTURE

When man, the earth-bound, in his pride,
Put gravitation's law aside,
And dared the eagle's airy space,
So near to God's uncovered face,
In his vainglorious delight
That he had mastered human flight,
(Still dumb, and brother to the ox),
He opened a Pandora's Box.

Now with his science and his art
He's probed the atom's secret heart,
Releasing unimagined power
That may redeem him or devour.
And thus has man, still dumb and blind,
(Whose soul is smaller than his mind)
Flung wide, with one stupendous yell,
The doors of heaven, the gates of hell.

BABYLON

The walls of Babylon were high,
  And very great,
With towers reaching to the sky,
  Defying fate.
But Babylon is in the dust,
Her works into oblivion thrust,
And all we know of her is just
  Her name and date.

The kings of Babylon were rich,
  And very proud,
And sat erect on thrones at which
  The people bowed.
But kings and thrones and bowing slaves
Have found alike their common graves
Where now the mighty forest waves
  And fields are plowed.

We build new Babylons today
  With stolen gold,
And think they will not pass away
  Like that of old.
But someone of a later race
Will dig in some deserted place
And find on some stone's broken face
  Our story told.

QUATRAIN

My old God loved like a miser,
  And hated as men might hate.
My new God is better and wiser,
  And patient and poised and great.

THE RIVER AND THE SEA

Adown the patient stream of Time,
  In Life's impatient little boat,
Through scenes both awful and sublime
  My lonely spirit is afloat.
And on this river's moving crest
There is no place to stop and rest;
  From empty night to hungry dawn
  I must go on and on and on.

There is no one to take my place
  When I am fainting at the wheel,
To steer the boat along its race,
  Or fend the dangers from its keel.
The light that leads me through the dark
Has faded to a tiny spark,
  And just to keep that spark alive
  I have to strive and strive and strive.

But every river has an end,
  And every struggle has to cease,
And somewhere I shall find a friend,
  And somewhere I shall be at peace.
When I shall reach the broad and free
Still waters of Death's silent sea,
  With folded hands across my breast,
  I then shall rest and rest and rest.

DAY AND NIGHT

It's very strange that day will break
When slightest fall it does not take,
And stranger still that night can fall
And somehow never break at all.

203

ROOM-MATES

My feet live here in a small house;
   My heart goes out and in;
And my stay-at-home feet never know
   Where my travelling heart has been.

MY OLD SCHOOL READER

There's no book in all creation
   That has ever been in print
That can strike the fire of feeling
   From old memory's rusty flint
Like the dear old ragged Reader
   That I studied long ago
In the old log cabin schoolhouse
   When I went to Beaver Creek;
When we all took turns at reading
   As we sat there in a row,
And I kept my eye on Sally
   And the dimple in her cheek.

I have found it in the garret
   In an old forgotten trunk,
As I rummaged all the evening
   Over thirty years of junk,
And I dusted off the covers
   And I brought it to my room
To renew the old acquaintance
   And to ponder on the past.
Ah, how well my nose remembers
   That old delicate perfume
That has clung about its pages
   Ever since I saw it last!

Ripened in the dust of silence,
    Mellowed with the charm of age,
How my childhood whispers to me
    From each well-remembered page!
Ah, the stories and the pictures
    That I hadn't seen for years—
How they rise and stand before me
    Like the ghosts of happy days!
How they fill my heart with longing
    And my eyes with truant tears
For the schoolmates and companions
    Who have gone their silent ways!

LEISURE

He is always in a hurry,
    Running here and running there;
He is always full of worry,
    He is always full of care.

Looking after interests many
    Keeps him ever on the run,
And of time he hasn't any,
    So he misses lots of fun.

He is rich and getting richer;
    He is puffing up with pride;
But I've seen a common ditcher
    Who was better satisfied.

He can never stop a second
    For the greeting of a friend,
And it seems as if he reckoned
    That his rush will never end.

But at last the hurry ceases
　　And the day begins to dawn
When his nerves are shot to pieces
　　And his good digestion gone.

'Tis a sign that must be heeded;
　　Soon some leisure will be found.
He'll have all the time that's needed
　　Just to slumber in the ground.

THE KING IS DEAD

Oh, what are the kingdoms that rise,
Or the tottering kingdoms that fall,
　　When Eternity stands
　　With a rule in her hands
To measure the worth of it all?

Oh, what is a moment of fame,
And power that suddenly flies?
　　And what is a crown
　　When its credit is down?
And what is a king when he dies?

A king in the prime of his power
May bend the world to his will;
　　But a king in the grave
　　Is no more than a slave,
As he lies there stark and still.

But the wicked old world moves on,
And the mourners will soon forget.
　　New suns will arise
　　In the royal skies
When the earlier suns have set.

MYSTERY

I must not tell—for words would surely fail—
    The glamorous sweet magic of the pines,
Nor how across the breadth of hill and dale,
    Too dear for speech, a lambent glory shines.

But when I see, through something more than sight,
    The Mystery that has no other name,
My heart goes racing in its wild delight,
    And all my soul burns in me like a flame.

A WOMAN

She followed not the lure of fame
    Nor any high and vain ambition;
To live and serve without a name—
    That was her only thought and mission.

When she was young and in her prime
    She got no polished education.
She never wasted any time
    In running after wealth or station.

She kept herself in good repute—
    Ignored the fads and shunned the vices;
And future years will see the fruit
    Of her unselfish sacrifices.

She had no knowledge of the creeds;
    For argument she never lusted,
But simply left her future needs
    With God, whose providence she trusted.

If friends were thoughtless or untrue,
    She answered not with cruel railing,
But passed along and smiled and threw
    Love's mantle over every failing.

When others fell from day to day,
    Or stood condemned of willful sinning,
She tried to brush their stains away
    And help them make a new beginning.

She was no saint with upward gaze,
    The kind that only lives in fiction;
But in so many common ways
    Her life was all a benediction.

So when at last this woman slept—
    Whose touch had been so warm and human—
They gathered at her grave and wept
    And said, "The world has lost a woman."

THE SOUL OF A SONG

Oh, they come to me now from the weather-worn dwelling
    As it nestles alone 'mid the trees bending low,
And my heart is again with the old home-love swelling
    To the echo of songs that I heard long ago.

Oh, they say that the old songs are gone out of fashion,
    And they strive to forget them and drive them away;
But I feel for those old friends a heart-thrilling passion
    That I never can feel for the songs of today.

There's a shadow of doubt and an inkling of science
    That pervades every tone of the new-fashioned song;
There's a want of true love and a lack of reliance
    On the great plan of nature that's faithful and strong.

I have oftentimes heard that the sweet sainted spirits
     Ever watch o'er the lives of the children of men,
And the soul that's in unison with them inherits
     All their wisdom and strength for life's struggle again.

And I think that the truth in the world of immortals
     Is the truth in the kingdom of music no less;
For the soul of a song enters in through the portals
     And is sung by the angels in heaven, I guess.

So I sit here alone by the slow-dying embers,
     And rejoice in the strength of each wonderful tone,
And I smile to myself as a man who remembers
     All the beautiful things that he ever has known.

Written at age 20.

MEMORIES

Sweet Memory, take my hand in thine
     And lead me gently through
The mystic ways of former days
     That my young fancy knew.

Oh, let me steal away with thee
     To days forever gone,
And let me feel again the zeal
     Of childhood's golden dawn.

The empty schoolhouse lonely stands
     Upon the wooded hill.
Its inmates gay have roamed away;
     Their noisy feet are still.

I pause upon the battered step
    That marks the silent door,
And sadly here I drop a tear
    For those I see no more.

I see within the dusky room
    Their names upon the wall,
And from the floor they walk no more
    The strange, wild echoes call.

And drifting down the shadow'd way
    That seems so sad and long,
I hear again the glad refrain
    Of childhood's early song.

O'er many a golden head I watch
    The sunlight dart and gleam.
The shadows pass, and then, alas!
    'Tis all a transient dream.

O sacred visions of delight,
    I bless ye, one and all,
For sunny skies and beaming eyes
    That ye so oft recall.

SECRETS

Oh, there be things that I would keep
    Forever secret in my soul,
But forth into the light they leap,
    And spread beyond my poor control.

And there be thoughts that I would tell
    To all creation's utmost reach;
But hidden in my heart they dwell—
    I cannot coax them into speech.

MAN OF THE PRESENT

I am the man of the present;
  The future will pass me by,
And somebody else will suffer,
  And somebody else will die.

But I will have paid my forfeit
  And purchased my long, long rest,
While somebody else is troubled
  With being the world's new guest.

The man who will come hereafter—
  So modern his time will be
That he will be moved to pity
  Whenever he thinks of me.

For I will be lost in shadows,
  So much a companion of shades,
And covered with such oblivion
  That memory almost fades.

"How curious," he will be saying,
  "How utterly strange and odd,
That this one time was a human,
  Which now is a lifeless clod!

"How strange to have been so ancient,
  And buried so long ago
That lands and times and seasons
  And lost in the changing show.

"But I am the man of the present.
  Of me it will never be said
That I lived in an age forgotten
  And slept with the nameless dead.

"For I am the man of the present—
    The very last word in date.
All dead men came too early,
    And others will be too late.

"Back-numbered and all out-moded
    Are they who have gone to sleep;
But I am the man of the present,
    And I have a date to keep."

But he will be dated and buried,
    And time will go over his head,
Till some other man of the present
    Has found him a long time dead.

POSTERITY

The nurse held out, in view of all,
A fluffy bundle, soft and small,
And turned the blanket to disclose
A very tiny mouth and nose.

A mouth and nose all pink and red,
And then an almost hairless head.
Two tiny fists came from the pack,
Opened and close, and folded back.

The others looked with all their eyes,
And made remarks that sounded wise;
But all they saw on that great night
Was just one helpless human mite.

I looked, the same as all the rest,
But what I thought was not expressed,
And what I saw would much surprise
Those seeing only with their eyes.

I saw, as in a vision dim,
That infant's issue follow him,
Till in a hundred years or two
I marvelled at the train he drew.

As, birth by birth, the family tree
Its branches spread from sea to sea;
So, death by death, the headstones rose
In numbers such as no man knows.

A child was born, the people said—
An infant in its mother's bed;
But no one seemed to be aware
That endless multitudes were there.

Wrapped in that pink and purple skin,
New nations waited to begin,
And, flowing from that single birth,
Its bloodstream tinctured all the earth.

TROUBLE IN THE SHOP

Tonight there will be trouble in the shop,
And linotype will stop,
And operators, waiting for a clue,
Will wonder what to do.

The telegraphic stuff will all be in,
And no more yarns to spin,
And no more tales of interest or worth
From any where on earth.

The plates will all be stereotyped, I guess,
And maybe on the press,
Except the Editorial Page must wait,
Because this poem's late.

The make-up man, in such a time of doubt,
Will let his pipe go out,
While nervously he fingers brass and lead
To make the pieces spread.

'Twixt editorials and scissored stuff
There isn't quite enough.
An empty space about six inches long
Is yawning for a song.

The editor will light his last cigar
And order out his car,
And go home suddenly at noon of night,
Just mad enough to fight.

I know they'll saddle me with all the blame,
And say it is a shame
To keep the paper waiting all night through,
But nothing else would do.

I will confess it surely is a slam!
I'm sorry—yes I am!
The song would not develop very fast,
But here it is at last.

SEA-WIND

A little lonely sea-wind,
    Lost along the shore,
Calling for companions
    That answer nevermore.
They have gone and left it
    In their hurried flight—
Left it wet and wailing
    In the gloomy night.

214

A little friendly sea-wind
    That loitered far behind,
Picking up the sea-sounds,
    All that it could find;
Picking up the voices
    Of all the little waves
That ran before it weeping
    From the sad sea-graves.

A little weary sea-wind
    With arms so full of grief,
And no one thinks about it
    Nor comes to its relief.
It calls for its companions;
    They do not hear its cries;
And there upon the sea-sand
    It settles down and dies.

SMILE

Somebody told a homely child
That she was pretty when she smiled,
And something in her bosom stirred
Responsive to the friendly word.

The little girl was very quick
To learn that little smiling trick,
And all the ugly took its flight
Before her beaming new delight.

Next day the neighbors saw her pass,
And said, "Who is that lonely lass?
And where's that homely little jane
That used to amble down the lane?"

215

LET ME PUT YOU IN A SONG

You who stand at beauty's portal—
    Oh, the future is so long!
Let me make your youth immortal—
    Let me put you in a song.

Laugh in this your day of laughter;
    Dream in this your dreaming hour;
Years and years will follow after;
    Frost will touch the tender flower.

But if you'd stay young and golden,
    If you'd never know decline,
Let yourself be caught and holden
    In this little song of mine.

Oh, the calendar is clever,
    But beware its lying tongue!
I will make you live forever,
    And my song will keep you young.

NOCTURNE

The lengthening shadows fade. The Sunset gold
Is dim on field and fold,
And creatures weary of their day-time quest
Turn homeward, seeking rest.

O hushed and holy falls the sacred dusk,
With scents of myrrh and musk,
And healing silence follows the loud day,
Till grief is dreamed away.

LIGHTS AND SHADOWS

A medley of lights and shadows,
    And the busy world spins 'round;
Glad souls there be, and sad ones,
    But each soul outward-bound—
Breathed out from the Source of Being
    To wander while through space,
The dupe of consuming passions
    Or the object of saving grace.

Glad songs and the voice of laughter
    In many a gleaming hall,
And then the shroud and the death-watch
    And the funeral's dismal pall.
A season of strength is given
    Wherein we shall all be gay,
But the pallor of death comes after,
    And the desolate dreamless clay.

THE CONQUEROR

Spake the City to the Forest:
    "Your retirement I demand!
Get you up into the mountain,
    That my greatness may expand!"

Meekly did the Forest answer:
    "Master, Master, I depart!
But I'll come again and gather
    My possessions to my heart."

So the City, striding forward
    In its brick-and-mortar strength,
Drove the Forest on before it
    All the teeming valley's length.

217

There the Forest stood and waited
    While the long years came and went—
Waited with prophetic patience
    Till the centuries were spent.

Lo, the brick-dust in the valley,
    Where great walls have melted down!
And the passing stranger wonders
    If that used to be a town.

Now the dust is veined with rootlets
    Where the mold is rich and black,
And the green that shows above it
    Is the Forest coming back.

THE MASTER MUSICIAN

The voice of every living thing
    Is held a captive in his hand,
And from his subtle finger-tips
    The rapid rolling thunder speaks.
The first glad notes are those that tell
    Of life among the rich and grand,
And then I hear the muffled sound
    Wherein the soul of sorrow reeks.

I do not see the master's form
    Nor yet the instrument he plays;
I am not conscious of the fact
    That all the world of sight and sound
That pulses in my inner soul
    And fills my raptured mental gaze
Could be the handiwork of man
    And in so small a compass bound.

The old piano shrieks and groans
  In agony of hopeless woe,
And tragic scenes come into view
  Beneath the master's witching hand;
And silent fleets of phantom ships
  All rudderless and aimless go
On bottomless and shoreless seas
  To port in some far phantom land.

JOURNEY'S END

Somewhere along the winding trail,
  When I am all too tired to weep,
I'll lay life's little toys aside
  And go to sleep.

It makes no difference after that
  How long or short the passing night.
Whatever comes or doesn't come
  Will be all right.

To him on whom the narrow house
  Has but a moment closed its door,
A million ages, more or less,
  Will be no more.

I will not question nor complain,
  Nor issue orders to the skies.
I'm trusting God to keep me safe,
  For He is wise.

If He intends to wake me up,
  I'll like it just as well as you;
But if He lets me slumber on.
  That's all right, too.

THE DEATH OF A CENTURY
December 31, 1900

Let a solemn prayer be said,
    And let holy incense rise;
Weave ye garlands for the dead,
    For tonight a Century dies.

Let a funeral bell be toll'd
    When the evening sun is low;
For the Century is old.
    And it's time for it to go.

Nineteenth Century, from thee,
    All these fateful hundred years,
Came our privilege to see
    Happy smiles and bitter tears.

But thy last and final flight
    Has been heralded afar,
And thou goest out tonight
    Like the fading of a star.

FORMULA

Great men, great men, learned and wise,
Have you any secret from the far, far skies?
Have you any formula, tried and true,
That nobody understands but you?

Wise men, wise men, steeped in lore,
Have you any key to the magic door?
Have you any pass-word, mystic, deep,
That I, even I, might learn and keep?

220

Strong men, strong men, muscled and thewed,
Where do you get your powerful food?
Have you any garden in some hid glen
That grows good living for mighty men?

Great men, wise men, strong men all,
This is the cry of the weak and small.
Tell me the secret and give me the sign,
And let your power be also mine.

HARD ROAD

When the road was level and smooth and wide,
And we all had courage and strength and pride,
We ran, each man in his own free way,
For the prize that out in the distance lay.

We felt no need of the clasping hand
Of a faithful friend who would understand;
But flushed with victory—selfish—proud—
We hurried ahead with the hurrying crowd.

But now—oh, now—when the hills are steep,
And the pitfalls yawn and the strong men weep,
We are thankful and glad, as we stumble and drift,
For a friendly hand that will give us a lift.

ANTE-POST-MORTEM

There's always something to be said
In praise of people who are dead;
But, living, they are subject first
To being criticized and cursed.

221

SATAN'S FALL

They tell me that once when the devil was young,
   And the earth hadn't sprung into view,
He dwelt up in heaven the angels among,
   And appeared to be holy and true.
   And appeared to be righteous and true;
That he walked with the angels and sang in the choir
   And appeared to be perfect and true.

But he got contrary and wouldn't do right,
   And was momently—instantly—hurled
From his beautiful throne in the regions of light
   To the uttermost end of the world;
   To the thithermost end of the world;
To a sulphurous lake at the farthermost side
   Of the nethermost end of the world.

ALTER-EGO

There is said to be a poor old man
   Bearing my name,
Who walks the world in weariness,
   Covered with shame.

I think I have seen that man
   On a back street,
Ragged and bent and starved,
   And nothing to eat.

His face was like my face,
   Only it couldn't smile,
And he stood there looking at me
   For a long while.

VULNERABLE

A man may build about his heart
   A strong defense of triple steel,
   And boast within himself and feel
Secure from every coming dart.

But, lo! his boasted strength is vain,
   For when he sees no danger nigh,
   An arrow from a woman's eye
Shall cleave his armor all in twain.

SACRAMENT

As night began to gleam,
I fared me forth to roam
About the hills of home,
Where walk, with silence shod,
Above the greening sod,
The glorious feet of God.

I saw a friendly toad
Creep out from his abode
And hop across the road.
I heard a cricket's call
Somewhere behind a wall—
Just once, and that was all.

But there a feast was spread
At which my soul was fed
With heaven's holy bread;
Which did such joy afford
As when, at heaven's board,
The wine of life is poured.

TO A CLOUD

O beautiful feathery cloud,
    You're just in the shape of a wing,
And the night groweth late
While I listen and wait
    To see if an angel will sing.

O angel, I know you are there,
    For two little stars are in view;
They are just the right size
For your beautiful eyes,
    And it's easy to recognize you.

But now you have covered your face
    And hidden the light of your eyes;
And I can't see a thing
But the point of your wing
    As it vanishes out of the skies.

CHOICE

Away back yonder when years were few,
We fell a-talking of what we'd do;
Away back yonder when years were long,
You chose money and I chose song.

You bought a farm and a mansion grand,
But all you got was the house and land.
The green of the meadow, the blue of the sky
Were mine for the taking as I went by.

You bought a bird's nest in a tree,
But all the birds belong to me.
You bought a hill with splendid views;
You bought a sunset you can't use.

You've got money—an awful pile—
But that won't pay for a baby's smile.
You've got power in mill and mart—
I've got happiness in my heart.

You pay the taxes and meet the bills,
But I take the beauty of all your hills
And weave it into a splendid song
To gladden the world as it moves along.

You'll go strutting in garments fine,
Pitying me in these rags of mine.
I'll go hungry and you'll have bread,
But I'll be a great man when I'm dead.

MEMORY'S SWEETS

With the passing of time we are sure to forget
The annoying things and the moments that fret;
And when memory's power is put to the test,
We remember the things that are sweetest and best.

A LAZY CROWD

Thoreau was a lazy man long years ago;
   Burroughs had a slow gait that hustlers condemn;
Riley wasn't much account, as all men know,
   And I'm another sorry cuss, just like them.

FULFILLMENT

I sought the doubtful comfort of my grief
    Wherewith to meet Time's annual disaster;
For I was burdened with the falling leaf,
    And subject to the wind as to a master.

All winter long my heart was in the grave,
    Doubtful of life and all departed glory;
Unmindful that the naked trees were brave
    And still believed the resurrection story.

But now I have no cynic's word to say,
    As Time fulfills her old perpetual pledges;
As, inch by inch and day on growing day,
    The green creeps back along the wintered hedges.

AUTUMN FIRES

Let this be noted as we pass:
    The maple wears a flaming coat;
And death has touched the aged grass,
    And crickets sound a sadder note.

All day the far blue hills are fed
    With fainter light from weaker sun;
And, mourning where their loves lie dead,
    The late leaves redden one by one.

Old chimneys wake with autumn fires,
    And send aloft their curling breath;
And long-dead ghosts of old desires
    Walk nightly in their robes of death.

I WILL BE A HERMIT

I will be a hermit in an old grey town,
  With an old volume and a warm hearth-fire;
With a lit candle when the night comes down—
  These be the heaven of my desire.

I will have a garden when the spring days wake,
  Ready for to dig to an old-time song;
I will have a grapevine tied to a stake;
  I will have a bean-row ten yards long.

CONTACT

My friend is living in a distant land,
But any moment I may touch his hand
  And feel his pulsing heart.
My enemy is dwelling at my door,
But I may never know him any more,
  For we are worlds apart.

GOSSIP

Love had a date
  At Beauty's bower,
And Joy was gotten
  In a glad hour.

A funny little breeze
  Went laughing by,
And there was a twinkle
  In the Dawn's eye.

LITTLE THINGS

If I cannot be a sea.
    Surely I can be a spring.
Surely, with refreshing flow,
To some traveller old and slow,
Close beside me bending low,
    I can some small comfort bring.

If I cannot be a sun,
    Surely I can be a star.
Surely, with my little ray,
I can light some mortal's way,
And the nearer darkness slay,
    If I cannot shine afar.

TWO GRAVES AT ASHEVILLE

Two graves at Asheville call me back
Along the rugged mountain track,
And each one holds my spirit's brother.
O. Henry—all his labor done—
Sleeps sweetly, peacefully, in one;
Tom Wolfe—he slumbers in the other.

AFFINITIES

If you were a blossom and I were a bee,
You might be growing beyond the sea,
But I'd fly over the waters blue
And find the meadow that sheltered you.

LINCOLN

The stuff God uses to make folks
    Is very common clay,
And constantly His furnace smokes—
    He moulds them every day.
But when the folks are made and done,
    As well as God can do,
Each one like every other one
    Is just like me and you.

The stuff God uses to make MEN
    Is very rare indeed,
And God can use it only when
    There is supremest need.
But when, with wise and careful strokes,
    God moulds a MAN in shape,
The whole creation full of folks
    Stands wondering and agape.

God saved and saved His precious stuff,
    While working out His plan,
Until at last He had enough
    To make another MAN.
And then, with sure and steady aim,
    The thunderbolt was hurled:
A great light out of darkness came,
    And LINCOLN filled the world.

ON MEETING A WOMAN POET

Already, on the printed page,
    I knew you for the queen of song,
And gladly did my tongue engage
    To hymn your praises season-long.

It was your soul that I addressed;
  I answered to your spirit's call.
What form and feature you possessed—
  I had not thought of them at all.

Now must I rue the fateful night
  That led me to a fateful place,
Where, glorious in the mellow light,
  I saw the wonder of your face.

I once your fellowship could claim
  With never thought of ill or harm.
Now, added to your poet's fame,
  I must endure your woman's charm.

And I, who have no wish to say
  So bold a thing to womankind,
Must steel my rebel heart and pray
  That God would make me beauty-blind.

SOUL OF POETRY

All things at all times
Can be fitted to rhymes,
And a blessing or curse
May be uttered in verse.

But a poem's high art
Is a something apart,
And it must be imbued
With a mystical mood.

It is wistful and wise,
With a touch of surprise,
And a deep-hidden vein
Of delectable pain.

230

It is beauty unguessed;
It is sorrow suppressed;
It is wonder made fair
By the breath of a prayer.

It is everything true
That the mighty gods knew
From eternity's dawn
Till the heavens are gone.

LOVE ME WHILE I LIVE

I will not ask that in the future years,
    When I have passed into that Silent Land,
Thou come to me with kisses and with tears
    And offer love—I would not understand.

I will not ask that wreathed flowers be brought
    To wither on my coffin and to die;
I would not that my name be proudly wrought
    On chisel'd shaft up-rising to the sky.

I need the comfort that thy smile would lend
    In the dark way that I must travel here;
But in that vale toward which my footsteps tend
    I shall not heed the falling of the tear.

So if thou hast a blessing to bestow,
    Or if thou hast a kindly word to give,
Defer it not till I am lying low
    In death's embrace, but tell me while I live.

THE KISS

You smiled, and my soul
 In a moment took fire,
And I could not control
 My o'erweaning desire
To fold you secure
 'Gainst my warm throbbing breast,
And kiss your demure
 Little lips into rest.

Reluctant you came,
 Like a coy young sprite,
With a blush as of shame
 Interwove with delight.
When I felt the soft touch
 Of your warm, wavy hair,
The sensation was such
 That I fainted right there.

But no man of the race
 Could unconscious remain
With the dream of your face
 Dancing over his brain.
So I came to myself
 In a moment of time,
And—I kissed you, sweet elf,
 And that kiss was sublime.

The wine may be rare
 That great Jupiter sips,
But it cannot compare
 With the wine of your lips.
For I never had known
 The full meaning of bliss
Till my lips met your own
 In that rapturous kiss.

MY CASTLE IN SPAIN

In sunny Spain, upon my broad estates,
I have a castle with an hundred gates.
My stately palms and cedars are astir
With all the gentle winds that never were.

Within, my halls and chambers are perfumed
With bright, perpetual flowers that never bloomed,
And dreamy maids by gallant knights are led
To banquet tables that were never spread.

WE TWO

We two shall make a feast of hearts
    And spread the tinted covers;
And when the painted revel starts,
We two shall play the leading parts,
And set the pace in loving arts
    For all the world of lovers.

We two shall dance exceeding well,
    And brim our lips with laughter;
Nor care what gods in heaven dwell,
Nor heed the tales that preachers tell
About the fabled fires of hell,
    Nor what shall come hereafter.

There shall be masters to provide
    The music rich and splendid;
But to that court of regal pride
The gift of peace shall be denied,
And we shall go unsatisfied
    When all the feast is ended.

Then will you, when the lights are low,
   And all the guests are leaving,
Turn with me from the empty show,
And forth into the desert go,
Till we are comforted with woe
   And satisfied with grieving?

A DROP OF DEW

There is a tiny blade of grass
   That grows upon a desert plain,
Away from where the rivers pass
   With borders dense of shrub and cane.

I saw it bow its head one night;
   I heard it pray, "O Heaven, do,
From thine abundance of delight,
   Please send me one sweet drop of dew."

My heart is like that blade of grass
   That sighs amid the summer heat;
It fain would tip love's magic glass
   And quaff it's nectar cool and sweet.

The holy heart of heaven bent
   In kind regard to heed the prayer,
And down the twilight shadows sent
   A mist of dew drops rich and rare.

And thus I know, my bonny lass,
   I could a life of bliss pursue,
Were I a tiny blade of grass
   And thou my only drop of dew.

THE FAR VIEW

Climb up the spangled sky-way till you see
   The earth stand out before you as a ball.
How smooth and perfect will the circle be!
   You will not see the saw-tooth hills at all.

So may the finished circle of my days
   Smooth out the staggers of my wayward feet,
And hide my blunders from the future's gaze,
   And make my half-done task appear complete.

A LYRIC OF LOVE

Come sit here by my side the while
   I sing my lyric to thee
Of all the empty days I met
   Before I ever knew thee.

Of all the aimless, empty days
   That crept so slowly by me,
With only vague, uncertain peace
   To promise—and deny me.

Before the light of angel eyes
   Drew heaven closer to me,
And banished all the clouds of doubt
   That erstwhile did pursue me.

Now let us hope that they are done—
   Those days of stormy weather—
And let us take each other's hand
   And march along together.

OH, TO BE MARRIED IN MAY

O Love, from the South returning,
   With all of your wandering o'er:
I give the glad hand of the dear native land,
   And bid you a welcome once more.
My love has been faithful and constant;
   I have dreamed of you night and day;
And, oh, the sweet bliss of the welcoming kiss,
   And, oh, to be married in May!

To have lived in the shadow of sorrow;
   To have seemingly loved in vain;
To have wept bitter tears through the joyless years—
   Through the pitiful years of pain.
And then to pass from the shadows
   And stand where the sunbeams play;
And, oh, the sweet charms of your circling arms.
   And, oh, to be married in May!

FIRST AND LAST

A brave young beau
   And a fair maid;
A light turned low,
   And a drawn shade.

A tale full old
   In the world's prime
Is once more told
   For the first time.

Give each true swain
   On the world's face
The joy or pain
   Of his own case,

The swains of old
   Have become nil;
Their loves are cold
   And their tongues still.

And what they spoke
   To their fair maids
Is gone in smoke
   As a dream fades.

There is no clue
   In the heart hid;
The present must do
   As the past did.

The swain today,
   When he has doubt,
Must feel his way
   Till he finds out.

It's just as new
   To the last pair
As to all those who
   Have been there.

And no man knows
   Till his heart speaks,
What things are those
   That the world seeks.

A brave man's vow,
   And a maid's kiss:
And silence now,
   And a great bliss.

DISILLUSION

If, in the vast economy of God,
One hungry little clod
Might make a wish and have it granted free,
This were the wish for me:

To be a child forever, and to keep
The joys of song and sleep—
To know again the splendid things I knew
When everything was true.

To have the wisdom of a dreaming boy,
When life was perfect joy,
Before the armies of encroaching doubt
Had put my faith to rout.

Alas, that disillusionment must come
And find us standing dumb
Before a broken idol of dead stone,
Wishing we had not known.

THE BICYCLE DOES NOT CHANGE

The bicycle craze in my boyhood days
    Is a thing I will never forget.
I was burnin' the pike with my pretty new bike,
    And the auto—it hadn't come yet.

Two wheels an' a frame that were always the same,
    An' a handle-bar stayin' just so;
An' a crank an' a chain that forever remain
    As they were half a century ago.

Then the gas buggy came, and it wanted a name,
    An' they called it the automobile.
An' it rattled along like somethin' was wrong,
    An' they couldn't keep air in the wheel.

Then the very next year they were changing the gear,
    An' a-addin' a new-fashioned hood;
Then a horn that was mute when you wanted to toot,
    An' a starter that wasn't no good.

But the bicycle stayed as originally made,
    An' the models are all just alike.
The pattern an' plan with which it began
    Is still good enough for the bike.

Now the streamlining fad has been going like mad
    Till the auto looks new and strange;
And the gadgets you find fairly addle your mind,
    But the bicycle does not change.

THE PASSING SHOW

The builders go; the building will not stay;
    There is no permanence that we can trust;
And under all foundations that we lay,
    The gnawing worm writes records in the dust.

We pitch our tent tonight on such a spot—
    One-night comedians with our mimic show.
The wheel of fortune turns, and we are not,
    And none will take account of where we go.

HELEN

Helen, when you're in my sight,
I am speechless with delight,
And my thoughts are all aflame
At the mention of your name.

Ah, your name! It may be true
That it's more your name than you
That intoxicates my brain
Like some heavenly refrain.

For the halo that you wear
Crowned another Helen's hair.
You, the heir of Homer's song,
In her shining wake belong.

With a less immortal name,
Would you quite have been the same?
Just imagine, if you can—
What if they had named you Ann?

VOICELESS

The little thoughts that settle into speech
    Grow commonplace and tiresome by and by,
While only those that lie beyond our reach
    Call forth the hungry heart's unending cry.

The little feelings that can be expressed
    Are just the surface ripples of the soul;
And buried deeper in the silent breast
    Lie vast uncharted seas beyond control.

THE UNSPEAKABLE

Can ever the tale be true,
  Or ever the song complete,
Though ever we worship the words that woo,
And tune the strings of our harp anew
  To a song full old and sweet?

Ah, never! The tongue is mute,
  And thought is a far-spent cry
That follows afar in vain pursuit
Where love's keen arrows of lightning shoot
  Across the fond heart's sky.

Alone in the lover's breast
  The riches of love must lie.
The faith and the fire, the zeal and the zest,
Must ever and ever remain unguessed
  By the proud world rolling by.

THE LAW OF THE EARTH

Life for life is the law of the earth;
Death for death is the price we pay.
Battle and bleed from the hour of birth
Back to the arms of the primal clay.

Only the seed that falls and dies
Lives again in the tender plant,
And the blood of a thousand murders cries
Through every life that the heavens grant.

The atom dies that the worm may live,
And the worm must die for the fowl to feast;
And the fowl, ere long, its life must give
To prolong the life of the hungry beast.

241

And then we follow the winding way,
With life and death in the mingled plan,
Till the beast his head on the block must lay
To feed the life of his master, man.

The soldiers march to the roll of drums
And many a battle is bravely planned,
And the fight goes on till the finish comes,
And men must fall that the State may stand.

UNANSWERED QUESTIONS

Around in ever-widening grooves—
    In curves and circles without end—
The perfect scheme of being moves,
    And men forever Godward tend.

And whether consciously we go,
    Or blindly, it is all the same;
The tides of life will ebb and flow—
    Our choice is nothing but a name.

Strive as we will to overcome
    The ancient law that holds us fast,
We find our human lips are dumb
    And voiceless in a scheme so vast.

God rules, and that is all we know;
    Our human minds reach out for more.
Our little thoughts may come and go,
    But truth is changeless as before.

The Power that in such wisdom planned
    And set each world within its place,
Can surely all results command,
    And every moving atom trace.

And we, as fragments of the whole,
 Cling helpless as the worlds revolve;
And all the problems of the soul
 Are things that we can never solve.

Why should we wear our lives away
 In useless cares that gain us naught,
Since God Omnipotent holds sway,
 Superior to our every thought?

God's will is the unchanging law
 That rules us if we wake or sleep;
And every movement He foresaw
 And shaped it from the formless deep.

We are but helpless lumps of clay,
 And plastic in His moulding hand,
And not until earth's final day
 May we these deep things understand.

FOR THE NEW YEAR

I want this year to be my best,
With all my better self expressed:
From day to day and week to week,
The life triumphant I would seek.

I want to feel each passing night
That I have spent the day aright,
So that no vain regrets may keep
My mind awake when I should sleep.

The life triumphant I would seek
From day to day and week to week;
With all my better self expressed,
I want this year to be my best.

MY NAME IN PRINT

My name has got away from me and gone
    Adventuring in magazines and books,
While I, in bashful modesty withdrawn,
    Observe unseen how confident it looks.

The name that clung to me in other years
    Is now an entity that dwells apart,
No longer subject to my hopes and fears,
    No longer burdened with my heavy heart.

I nursed its little life for many days,
    While oft it flickered like a dying flame;
But now it gets the glory and the praise,
    And I am just the servant of my name.

I stay at home and carry all the load,
    And do the heavy work and pay the bill.
My name goes out upon the glory road,
    But I'm the same old ignoramus still.

AN OFFICIAL QUAIL HUNT

Written while Calvin Coolidge was President

A certain Cal Coolidge, as you may have heard,
Went down in Virginia to shoot him a bird—
To shoot him a quail for to make him a pie,
For he's a good eater, and that is no lie.

He took him some clothes like the hunters all wear,
And he took him a gun that was loaded for bear,
And he took him a dog that was blooded and fine,
And a man to look after the precious canine.

He was careful to see there was nothing he lacked,
And it took him a week to get everything packed,
Which included provisions and music and books,
And a tent and a bed and a couple of cooks.

It seemed like a great preparation to make,
When only the life of a bird was at stake;
But Cal was determined to do it up right
If it took him from now till his whiskers were white.

So he went to Virginia, as I have remarked,
And found an old camp where some hunters had parked,
And he sent out his men to explore all around
And see if a partridge or two could be found.

When the birds had been found (for of course they
    were thick),
They didn't seem scared and they didn't look sick,
But sat around smiling, as much as to say:
"We're going to have fun in this medder today."

The President's typewriter, always at hand,
Was quickly set up on its portable stand,
And the President hammered out thousands of words
Of a state proclamation to read to the birds.

"Dear birds," it began, "I am not unaware
That life is as sweet to the birds of the air
As it is to a President out with a gun,
But a hard-working ruler has got to have fun.

"So I hope, my dear birds, that you are patriots true,
And can feel the great honor that's coming to you—
Of being shot down in your beautiful prime
By the mighty Cal Coolidge who wants a good time.

245

"Just think how the next generation of quails
Will stand at attention and twiddle their tails,
And boastfully tell in a voice of pride
How once their brave fathers had gloriously died.

"Now step out in line, like good soldiers will,
And stand close together and perfectly still,
And hold up your heads and draw in a deep breath,
And be thankful to meet such a glorious death."

Having written these lines, with a wave of his hand,
He summoned a flunkey and gave the command:
"Go read to the quails that you find in the field
This great proclamation, here solemnly sealed."

So the man took the paper and read it aloud,
And the birds never did look so happy and proud,
And they nodded their little brown heads for to say
That they quite understood and would gladly obey.

Now the great little ruler of forty-eight states
Was saddened, of course, when he thought of the fates
Of the beautiful birds he was going to slay,
But it had to be done, and with no more delay.

So he picked up the gun that was loaded for bear,
And he balanced it well on a stump that was there,
And he dropped to his knees and he took a fine sight,
And he pulled on the trigger with all of his might.

The gun went off like a war-time bomb
And shocked that President deaf and dumb,
And it kicked him back in a broomstraw pile,
Where he lay and grunted for a right smart while.

Not a bird was touched, not a feather flew,
But they all sat lined up just as true,
As if they waited for one more shot
To see if Callie could hit the spot.

The shot went over the birds, somehow,
And shot off the horns of a muley cow
As she grazed in a meadow of timothy hay
On another plantation two miles away.

WHEN DE FIRE TROMP SNOW

Hear dat crackin' an' crunchin' sound
    When de fire tromp snow!
Jis' like walkin' on snowy ground,
Big flakes flutterin' all around—
Mighty shore sign, Ise allers found,
    When de fire tromp snow.

Bettah be makin' dem cows a bed
    When de fire tromp snow.
Pile more leaves in de empty shed,
An' see 'at dey's fodder up overhead.
Gwine er be weather 'at folks 'll dread,
    When de fire tromp snow.

Bettah be huntin' dem overshoes,
    When de fire tromp snow.
Ain't got very much time to lose
Er-gettin' dat overcoat out to use,
If you am a-wantin' to 'scape dem Flues,
    When de fire tromp snow.

Bettah be sawin' dat old wood-pile
　　When de fire tromp snow.
Ain't goin' ter be but a little while
Till big backlogs will be in style,
An' plenty of pine will make you smile,
　　When de fire tromp snow.

Bettah be layin' dem raisins in
　　When de fire tromp snow;
Bettah look inter de tater bin
An' see dey's enough ter fill yer skin
Till all dat snow gits off agin,
　　When de fire tromp snow.

LUCILE

The love that once thou gavest me
　　I hold in sacred trust;
My vows I'll twine in the lonesome vine
　　That wanders above thy dust.

No other love can win my heart;
　　'Tis buried deep with thine;
It will not bow to the music now,
　　Nor the flow of Egyptian wine.

I loved thee more than life, Lucile;
　　I wept in the bitter hour
When death lay cold on thy locks of gold
　　And scorned me with its power.

For we had grown up side by side,
    And like of thought were we;
Our friendship grew to a love more ture
    Than love was known to be.

But dark, with the passing of thy smile,
    The radiant morning grew;
Soft words of cheer to my pulseless ear
    Were senseless jargon too.

When I would joy in what of good
    The passing seasons bring,
I remember in tears that the cruel years
    Were all too swift of wing.

And thus bereft of every tie
    That bound me unto time,
In silence I bow by thy sepulchre now
    And weave this mournful rhyme.

GRANDCHILDREN

Five stalwart sons my neighbor had,
And my five daughters made me glad;
And from their childhood it was said
Our children should each other wed.

Much did I think how it would be
To hold grandchildren on my knee,
And have, when I must journey hence,
A sort of patriarchal sense.

My neighbor's sons, it is revealed,
Are dead upon some battlefield,
And my fair daughters will grow old
With no offspring for me to hold.

What crime is this, that in life's list
A generation must be missed—
Five stalwart sons untimely dead,
And five fair daughters still unwed?

Poems of Protest

THE SURPLUS

We had "too much" of everything
    To wear and eat;
Of wool and cotton, silk and shoes,
    And corn and wheat,
And beans, potatoes, eggs and fruit,
    And milk and meat.

The bins were bursting on the farms
    Throughout the West,
And not a chance to use it all,
    To do our best;
We'd have to waste a little more,
    And burn the rest.

And so the word was passed around
    To great and small
That we must plant a smaller crop,
    Or none at all,
And so keep down the harvest yield
    The coming fall.

The hungry people swarmed the streets
    And country lanes,
And bummed their way on motor trucks
    And cattle trains,
And often fired a borrowed gun
    Into their brains.

We could have found out long ago,
    By taking heed,
That hunger, nakedness, and all
    Their hateful breed,
Come from "too much" of everything
    That people need.

DEVILUTION

Beginning near the dawn of time,
   When all the seas were warm,
A protozoa in the slime
   Begat a living form.

It was a very little mite,
   But all that we could wish.
It went ahead one rainy night
   And got a flying fish.

The flying fish became a bird,
   As all the books agree;
And after that, was seen and heard
   A monkey in a tree.

The monkey was so full of pride,
   He studied out a plan,
And he was never satisfied
   Till he became a man.

As soon as man on earth appeared,
   He hunted him a cave,
And growled and muttered through his beard
   And said that he was brave.

He didn't make the cave, but, oh,
   He spied it from a limb,
And he would have the world to know
   That it belonged to him.

All other men who hadn't caves
   Must stay out in the cold,
And they must be his humble slaves
   And do as they were told.

He found a place where berries grew,
  And trees with nuts galore;
He claimed the nuts and berries too,
  And still he wanted more.

To own creation was his aim,
  And though it wasn't right,
He went ahead and filed a claim
  On everything in sight.

He made himself a mighty king
  And ruled with iron hand,
And took his toil of everything
  That grew upon the land.

The slaves went out at dawn of day
  And gathered goodly store,
And brought the treasures back to lay
  Before the master's door.

The master, he was full of biz,
  And made his servants pay.
"He claims it, and I guess it's his,"
  Was all that they could say.

They bowed and kissed his garment's hem
  And thought the homage due.
It never once occurred to them
  To do some "claiming" too.

When men began to ask for laws
  Endangering his reign,
He staged a war for "freedom's cause"
  And had the people slain.

And thus the captains and the kings
  Have made themselves secure,
And brought about a state of things
  That men cannot endure.

They've fastened on the heavy yokes
    And piled the burdens high,
And made the lives of common folks
    One bitter wailing cry.

They've made the earth a howling hell,
    A reeking den of strife,
A place unfit for men to dwell,
    And men are tired of life.

The men today upon the earth
    Admit the show is bum;
They haven't got their money's worth,
    And wish they hadn't come.

But they go out a-hunting wives
    On whom to lay the blame,
And start a gang of other lives
    To go and do the same.

And every link along the chain
    Increases as it goes,
And doubles up the sin and pain,
    And multiplies the woes.

Today the human current runs
    As blindly as before,
Still getting more unhappy sons
    To suffer and get more.

They could have stopped it long ago
    If they had only tried,
And got no other sons of woe
    Till all of these had died.

If men would quit begetting men
    Till human birth could cease,
The race would soon die out, and then
    The world would be at peace.

But even that were not enough,
    For, being rid of men,
That primal protozoa stuff
    Might start it all again.

THE TEMPTER

There is a tale that people tell—
    A tale that some have dared dispute—
How Satan came up out of hell
    And tempted Eve with pleasant fruit.

But I have wondered if it might
    Have been the other way around—
That Eve, the Temptress, took delight
    In some new power she had found.

No devil's lure could lay restraint
    Upon her charms of face and limb;
And Satan may have been a saint
    Until the woman tempted him.

HARDWARE

Away with Thought and all its fruits!
    No room for thinker or for sage!
The smooth "go-getter" only suits
    This cold, hard-driving business age.

No Milton gets a hearing now;
    No Emerson can win our thanks.
The only script that we allow
    Is something good at all the banks.

No modern Webster holds a crowd;
  No modern Clay can cause a thrill—
Unless his voice jingles loud
  Like dropping silver in a till.

God give us men whose bones consist
  Of standard automobile parts!
Whose brains are on the hardware list;
  Who have cash-registers for hearts.

RULERS

The fat old men foregathered
  In steel-and-concrete towers,
And shook their bags of money
  And boasted of their powers.

The lean young men went marching,
  The lonesome women cried;
And there was war and glory,
  And rest for those who died.

The fat old men made merry,
  With pomp and power increased,
And all the human vultures
  Were bidden to the feast.

Then up rose want and hunger,
  And death and foul decay;
They gnawed the firm foundations
  And all the house gave way.

Now there is fear and quaking
  In strong-built office chairs,
And rulers weep that vengeance
  Falls on them unawares.

A FEW LITTLE DURNS

In writing this thunder—
    These sermons and rhymes—
I have to think "dammit"
    A good many times.
But since that is cussing,
    A fellow soon learns
To make out with only
    A few little durns.

In reading the papers
    And watching the mess
The leaders are making,
    And all the distress,
I get so durn fretted,
    And tickled in turns,
I just have to let out
    A few little durns.

No matter how fretted
    And angry I am,
I always remember
    To never say damn.
But, oh, when my spirit
    With righteous wrath burns,
I need in my business
    A few little durns.

The durn politicians,
    And sky-pilots, too—
The leaders of fashion,
    And all the durn crew—
The gait they are going
    Most fittingly earns
The impressive rebuke of
    A few little durns.

Just "durn" isn't cussing,
    In moderate use—
No more than a snow-bird
    Is part of a goose.
When used by a man who
    For righteousness yearns,
I hope there's no harm in
    A few little durns.

Dear reader, be patient—
    I know it sounds rough;
But I am the fellow
    That's writing this stuff.
I know what is needed
    In these-here concerns,
And you must allow me
    A few little durns.

SUICIDE

It hurts to shoot into your brain;
    A high jump sets you reeling:
To be run over by a train
    Is not a pleasant feeling.

A rope will choke you, people say,
    And poison may not kill you;
And drowning is a messy way
    When water starts to fill you.

I do not mean to laugh or scoff,
    Be harsh or unforgiving;
But any way you shuffle off
    Is most as bad as living.

MY RIGHTEOUS WRATH IS A-B'ILIN'

I'd like to always wear a grin,
   An' keep right on a-smilin';
But there's so much of crime an' sin
A-floatin' 'round where I have been,—
So many brutes in human skin—
   My righteous wrath is a-bilin'.

I'd like to just be singing songs,
   With blessin's 'round me pilin';
But when I see the passin' throngs
Of proud conceits an' boastful wrongs—
The Lie set up where Truth belongs—
   My righteous wrath is a-bilin'.

I'd like to think that there was not
   One trace of sin's defilin';
But when the Truth has gone to pot—
The devil crowned an' Christ forgot,
I can't help gittin' sorter hot—
   My righteous wrath is a-bilin'.

PATRIOTISM

Tommy Dubb was a German's son,
   And Jimmy Dubb was French,
And they both shouldered an army gun
   To die in a bloody trench.

The interests of Tom and Jim
   Were just about the same;
Each had a master over him
   Who understood the game.

261

These two had labored side by side,
　　And no disputes arose.
You could not, even if you tried,
　　Imagine them as foes.

But, lo! A bunch of royal scrubs
　　Among themselves had fussed;
And just for that a million Dubbs
　　Must bravely bite the dust.

So Tom and Jim rose up in haste,
　　As all good soldiers do,
And with their loaded guns they faced
　　And shot each other through.

IF YOU WANTED ME TO

O Lord, if I knew that You wanted me to,
　　I'd be willing to wait
For that splendid abode at the end of the road—
　　At the Beautiful Gate.

I would beg in the street for permission to eat
　　Of the husks and the crumbs.
I would sleep in the park when the nights are dark
　　Till the Great Day comes.

In the cold and the damp I would go as a tramp
　　Down the railroad track
With a song in my throat and a tattered old coat
　　To cover my back.

O Lord, I'd agree to have nothing, and be
　　Robbed of all my due,
And await my reward till the Day of the Lord—
　　If You wanted me to.

But who has been sent from Your battlement
　　With a word to say?
And why should I trust in old Greed and Lust?
　　Whose prophets are they?

O Lord, if You've planned to make me so great
　　In the By-and-By,
Can't I now have a taste of what's going to waste?
　　And if not, why?

THE MACHINES

The brawny men, the strong men, hairy-chested,
　　A week of stubble on their firm-set jaws,
Went daily to their work—they never rested—
　　And booming business moved without a pause.

Great whistles screamed, sudden and siren-throated;
　　Great chimneys belched their Amazons of smoke.
Contended songs across the ether floated,
　　While patient labor settled to its yoke.

Hath not the Maker said, by word of Moses,
　　That man shall labor, sweating for his bread?
So life on earth has been no bed of roses—
　　The hand must callous that the mouth be fed.

And this has been the law these countless ages—
　　Man's horny hands have grappled with his tools;
And life has bargained for its work and wages,
　　And always governed by the Boss's rules.

The Boss could figure like a math professor,
　　And had it down to fractions of a cent.
No Shylock he, and no hard-boiled oppressor—
　　He was that paragon, a business gent.

The toiling clod that reasoned not, nor studied,
   Nor had the sense to know his labor's worth—
Was not the whole creation filled and flooded
   With such poor crawling vermin of the earth?

Should he, the Boss, with brain and education,
   And wit to plan and execute his plans—
Should he not be exalted to a station
   Above the mob that labors with its hands?

A paycheck based upon the barest living
   That would sustain a human for a day,
And more than that there was no need of giving—
   And what could all the dumb-bell creatures say?

Enough today to buy tomorrow's gruel
   To give them strength to work ten hours more—
They would not think that vicious circle cruel,
   But bless the hand that brought it to their door.

They swarmed into the kingdoms of the Bosses;
   Servile and self-deluded did they come;
Not once suspecting all their heavy losses,
   Not once aware that they were very dumb.

But, oh, what weariness in brawn and muscle!
   What deadly tiredness in the dragging feet!
While still the whip of hunger made them hustle,
   And still the children clamored, "We must eat."

"God give us rest!" The people cried together,
   "A little rest from all this weary grind;
A day to ramble through the summer weather;
   A night to sleep, with troubles out of mind."

From all the mills as in a chorus spoken,
    Up-rose the universal pleading cry:
"We are slaves! We are terribly tired and broken!
    Oh, give us rest, or we will surely die."

The smart inventors had an inspiration—
    They'd make machines to do the work alone,
And not be bothered with the aggravation
    Of human hands that wear out to the bone.

And then the people, all so worn and troubled,
    Can go back home and get their needed rest,
While automatic profits can be doubled,
    And business go on booming at its best.

And so the work was hurried up and speeded,
    And got on better than it did before;
And so the new machines were all they needed—
    They didn't need the people any more.

But there was something very wrong about it—
    A curious blend of victory and defeat;
Because the idle people couldn't doubt it—
    Because the hungry people didn't eat.

The rich men groaned and filled the air with curses
    At all the piled-up goods from their machines;
The poor men cried aloud, feeling their empty purses,
    "How shall we buy, seeing we have no means?"

I RECKON IT'S RIGHT

I've wondered much at the way things go
In this old wobbly world below,
Where the man who toils from day to day
Has lots more debts than he can pay—
Always in a poverty-stricken plight—
    But I reckon it's right.

It seems so strange when we recall
That the man who does no work at all
Is the very chap who dresses fine
And goes to the best hotel to dine,
And gets his choice of all in sight—
    But I reckon it's right.

The poor old dirty son-of-a-gun
Who digs in the mine from sun to sun
Can't claim enough of the yellow dross
To pay his cruel and heartless boss
For a decent place to spend the night—
    But I reckon it's right.

I don't think God, in His heavenly plan,
Intended to rob the laboring man,
And give the wealth his hands produce
To the non-producing idler's use;
But they've improved God's plans a sight—
    And I reckon it's right.

CROSSES

As I went out walking all alone last night,
I saw a row of crosses in the pale moonlight.

I saw a row of crosses leading out from town,
And on across the river where the hill comes down.

Such tall black crosses as men use still,
Who crucify Gods on a shaken hill.

One time they fastened, by foot and hand,
A Power they never could understand.

They've done it again, to make wheels run,
With a million crosses instead of one.

The great wheels turn, and the message goes;
But what is the Power?   And nobody knows.

The same Lord God it well might be
That they once nailed to a cross-arm tree.

And it makes me wonder why men demand
Crosses for things they don't understand.

INTRODUCTION TO MY WORST POEM

The following piece of doggerel would not rate inclusion in this book except for the strange circumstance of its world-wide popularity during two World Wars. There will never be any way of knowing how many millions (or billions) of copies of it were circulated throughout the earth, but there is evidence that the figures were astronomical and then some.

The fact that the lines got printed anonymously in the home-town paper in December, 1944, gave me a chance to claim the authorship of the waif, and in doing so I wrote the paper a letter which I think is far better than the poem and therefore deserves to share the honors with it. Remember, this letter was written about December 22, 1944, while World War II was still going on.

With this further explanation, the poem and the letter are both printed here, and you may judge for yourself who it is that's nuts—me or this-here crazy world. Both, maybe?

WHEN THE WAR IS GOING TO END

Absolute knowledge have I none,
But my aunt's washer-woman's sister's son
Heard a policeman on his beat
Say to a laborer on the street
That he had a letter just last week,
Written in Latin—(or maybe Greek)
From a Chinese coolie in Timbucktoo
Who said that the Negroes in Cuba knew
Of a colored man in a Texas town
Who got it straight from a circus clown
That a man in Klondike heard the news
From a gang of South American Jews
About somebody in Borneo
Who heard of a man who claimed to know
Of a swell society female fake
Whose mother-in-law will undertake
To prove that her seventh husband's niece
Has stated in a printed piece
That she has a son who has a friend
Who knows when the War is going to end.

More About The Worst Poem

Mr. John Harden
DAILY NEWSettes
The Greensboro Daily News
Greensboro, North Carolina

Dear Mr. Harden:

Not that it matters very much, for I am not particularly proud of the performance; but just for the record I will say that I am the mute inglorious Milton who fathered that famous fugitive fragment of fine and fancy foolishness, "When the War Is Going to End," which you printed in our DAILY NEWSettes column on Saturday, December 2.

During the First World War, I was publishing in Western North Carolina a little free-lance humorous monthly sheet called *The Fool-Killer*. The paper turned out to be a remarkable success for a few years and reached a nation-wide paid-up circulation of 50,000 copies per month. I do not have the files of the paper before me as I write, and off-hand I can't be entirely sure of the date when the above-mentioned masterpiece was published, but my memory seems to insist on September, 1916, as the momentous date. Any way, I wrote the crazy rhyme to the possibility of its going beyond that.

But the issue was no sooner in the mails than I began to hear from it. From the four corners it came—copied and re-copied in all sorts of places. Clippings of it were sent me from everywhere, sometimes with my name attached, and often without it. The thing was obviously my poorest literary effort, but it turned out to be my most widely published and most famous production. Half the people you met had dog-eared copies of the thing stuck into their billfolds, and wouldn't you please let 'em read it to you?

Thus it went all over and all around this little old ball of mud during the First World War; and then, at the end of the war it got an honorable discharge and took a much-needed rest.

But when the Second World War started and people began to ask when it would end—well, my grand old masterpiece was just as good as new, and so it jined up and started on its globe-girdling rounds again. Since 1939, and especially since Pearl Harbor, it has been in action on all the battle-fronts. Every little while it gets wounded and has to go to the hospital and have its poetic feet operated on. But it never gives up.

Such is fame. Be a serious student of the classics. Soak yourself so full of the world's great poetry that it drips out at your eyes like thin molasses from a busted jug. Get down on your well-padded marrow bones and pray to all the merciful gods for an abundant helping of poetic inspiration. You feel inspired, uplifted and spiritually reborn. And while in this holy and happy state of mind and soul you write stuff that you know is darn good—stuff that ought to live at least a thousand years and earn you enough fame to reach from here to the New Jerusalem and back. But does your good stuff set the world on fire? Sorry, brother, but it does not. It comes limping back from one hard-boiled editor after another till it looks like the devil's dishrag on its way to the laundry, and you chuck it into the stove and cuss quietly and resolve that you will never write another line of poetry, so help you Pete.

And then here comes the doggonedest sorriest piece of drivel you ever did write, and it rings the bell for all the world to hear. Gets itself so well known in so many places all over the world that people don't know where it came from in the first place, and you get cheated out of the doubtful fame of being the poor cuss who wrote it. Wouldn't that burn you up? No wonder we poets are nuts.

Sincerely yours,
JAMES LARKIN PEARSON

271

INDEX

273

274

275

278